JAPANESE & ASIAN
50 LOW-FAT NO-FAT RECIPES

JAPANESE & ASIAN
50 LOW-FAT NO-FAT RECIPES

Exotic feasts without any of the fat; over 50 delicious
low-fat recipes shown in 250 stunning photographs

Edited by Jenni Fleetwood and Maggie Pannell

southwater

This edition is published by Southwater,
an imprint of Anness Publishing Ltd, Hermes House,
88–89 Blackfriars Road, London SE1 8HA;
tel. 020 7401 2077; fax 020 7633 9499

www.southwaterbooks.com; www.annesspublishing.com

If you like the images in this book and would like to investigate
using them for publishing, promotions or advertising, please visit
our website www.practicalpictures.com for more information.

UK agent: The Manning Partnership Ltd tel. 01225 478444;
fax 01225 478440; sales@manning-partnership.co.uk

UK distributor: Grantham Book Services Ltd tel. 01476 541080;
fax 01476 541061; orders@gbs.tbs-ltd.co.uk

North American agent/distributor: National Book Network
tel. 301 459 3366; fax 301 429 5746; www.nbnbooks.com

Australian agent/distributor: Pan Macmillan Australia
tel. 1300 135 113; fax 1300 135 103
customer.service@macmillan.com.au

New Zealand agent/distributor: David Bateman Ltd;
tel. (09) 415 7664; fax (09) 415 8892

ETHICAL TRADING POLICY

At Anness Publishing we believe that business should be
conducted in an ethical and ecologically sustainable way, with
respect for the environment and a proper regard to the
replacement of the natural resources we employ.
   As a publisher, we use a lot of wood pulp to make high-quality
paper for printing, and that wood commonly comes from spruce
trees. We are therefore currently growing more than 500,000
trees in two Scottish forest plantations near Aberdeen – Berrymoss
(130 hectares/320 acres) and West Touxhill (125 hectares/305
acres). The forests we manage contain twice the number of trees
employed each year in paper-making for our books.
   Because of this ongoing ecological investment programme, you, as
our customer, can have the pleasure and reassurance of knowing
that a tree is being cultivated on your behalf to naturally replace the
materials used to make the book you are holding.
   Our forestry programme is run in accordance with the UK
Woodland Assurance Scheme (UKWAS) and will be certified by
the internationally recognized Forest Stewardship Council (FSC).
The FSC is a non-government organization dedicated to
promoting responsible management of the world's forests.
Certification ensures forests are managed in an environmentally
sustainable and socially responsible basis. For further information
about this scheme, go to www.annesspublishing.com/trees

NOTES
Bracketed terms are intended for American readers.

For all recipes, quantities are given in both metric and imperial measures and,
where appropriate, in standard cups and spoons. Follow one set of measures,
but not a mixture, because they are not interchangeable.

Standard spoon and cup measures are level. 1 tsp = 5ml, 1 tbsp = 15ml,
1 cup = 250ml/8fl oz.

Australian standard tablespoons are 20ml. Australian readers should use
3 tsp in place of 1 tbsp for measuring small quantities.

American pints are 16fl oz/2 cups. American readers should use 20fl oz/
2.5 cups in place of 1 pint when measuring liquids.

Electric oven temperatures in this book are for conventional ovens. When using
a fan oven, the temperature will probably need to be reduced by about
10–20°C/20–40°F. Since ovens vary, you should check with your
manufacturer's instruction book for guidance.

The nutritional analysis given for each recipe is calculated per portion (i.e.
serving or item), unless otherwise stated. If the recipe gives a range, such as
Serves 4–6, then the nutritional analysis will be for the smaller portion size, i.e.
6 servings. Measurements for sodium do not include salt added to taste.

Medium (US large) eggs are used unless otherwise stated.

CONTENTS

INTRODUCTION

The majority of people living in Japan and East Asia have a very healthy diet, which is low in fat, high in fibre, with plenty of vegetables and relatively small amounts of meat. Much of their protein comes from fish and tofu, both of which are low-fat foods. Noodles and rice form the bulk of most meals, and processed foods are seldom eaten. In part, this diet evolved through necessity. Subsistence workers could not afford to eat large quantities of meat on a daily basis, even though pork, duck and chickens were – and still remain – an important part of the diet. Unfortunately, as countries like Japan and China have become increasingly prosperous, more fat is being consumed. In major cities like Tokyo, where individuals have adopted a more Western diet, the incidence of coronary heart disease is on the increase.

Some of the dishes exported to the West are none too healthy either. Kobe beef, a luxury food that is considered the foie-gras of beef and is heavily marbled with fat, is never going to make it to the list of best choices for optimum nutrition. Nor is the practice of deep-frying meat and vegetables to be recommended. There's been a lot of criticism of certain East Asian restaurants and takeaways in recent years, because of their devotion to the deep-fat fryer and their habit of slathering everything in thick, often very salty sauces, but such dishes – which are generally on the menu only because of Western demand – give a skewed picture of Asian cuisine.

Japan and East Asia can be a great source of very healthy, low-fat recipes. Asian cooks are fussy about what they eat, and ingredients are chosen with considerable care. Visit any open-air market and you will see cooks sifting through piles of gourds to choose one that is at just the right state of ripeness for the meal they have planned.

Right: Noodles add bulk and extra flavour to dishes without having a significant impact on fat levels. Fresh or dried egg noodles are available in various widths.

Meat and fish must be very fresh, a fact that can be a bit daunting to the visitor invited to choose their meal while it is still swimming in a tank, but which proves beyond any doubt that the item in question will not have far to travel to their table. This passion for freshness is particularly apparent – and important – if the fish is to be eaten raw, as it is in *sushi* and *sashimi*.

A HEALTHY WAY OF COOKING

Steaming and stir-frying are two of the most popular cooking methods in Japan and East Asia. Both these methods are ideal for the low-fat cook, since they require little or no oil to be used. The wok is the principal utensil. This extraordinarily versatile pan, with its rounded bottom, was originally designed to fit snugly on a traditional brazier or stove. Modern versions have flatter bases, to prevent wobble on electric stoves, but are still very efficient in the even way they conduct and retain heat. The sloping sides mean that the food always returns to the centre, where the heat is most intense.

Many of the woks on sale today are non-stick. Although traditional carbonized steel woks are the ones purists choose, because they are so efficient, non-stick woks are better for low-fat cooking, since they make it possible to stir-fry with the smallest amount of oil.

When stir-frying, the best technique is to place the wok over the heat without any oil. When the pan is hot, dribble drops of oil, necklace fashion, on to the inner surface just below the rim. As the drops slither down the pan, they coat the sides, then puddle on the base. You can get away with using just about a teaspoon of oil if you follow

Above: One of the reasons for cooking with fats is for flavour, but if you use aromatics like ginger (pictured) and garlic, there is no need to add oils or sauces for flavouring.

this method. Add the food to be cooked when the oil is very hot, and keep it moving. This is often done with a pair of chopsticks, but the easiest way is to use two spatulas or spoons, as when tossing a salad.

Add a metal trivet to a wok and it becomes a steamer. Better still, use a bamboo steamer. These attractive-looking utensils look rather like hat boxes, and come with tightly fitting domed lids. You can stack several tiers on top of each other over a wok partly filled with water. No fat will be needed and the food will taste delicious, with just a hint of fragrance from the bamboo.

A HEALTHY LIFESTYLE

Most of us eat fats in some form or another every day and we all need a small amount of fat in our diet to maintain a healthy, balanced eating plan. However, many of us eat far too much fat, and we should all be looking to reduce our overall fat intake, especially of saturated fats.

Regular exercise is also an important factor in a healthy lifestyle, and we should aim to exercise three times a week for a minimum of half an hour each session. Swimming, brisk walking, jogging, dancing, skipping and cycling are all good forms of aerobic exercise.

ABOUT THIS BOOK

This cookbook aims to bring you a wide selection of delicious and nutritious dishes from many regions of Japan and East Asia, all of which are low in fat, and are ideal to include as part of an everyday healthy and low-fat eating plan.

The book includes plenty of useful and informative advice. A short introduction gives a blueprint for healthy eating and has helpful hints and tips on low-fat and fat-free ingredients and cooking techniques. There are plenty of practical tips for reducing fat, especially saturated fat, in your diet, and the section on ingredients provides an insight into fruits, vegetables, flavourings and other essentials used in Japanese and East Asian cooking.

The tempting recipes – over 50 of them – will be enjoyed by all the family. They range from soups and appetizers to desserts and there are lots of delicious main course dishes for meat eaters and vegetarians. The emphasis throughout the book is on good food with maximum taste, and if you don't let on that the dishes are also low in fat, nobody is likely to guess.

Each recipe includes a nutritional breakdown, proving an at-a-glance guide to calorie and fat content (including saturated fat content) per serving, as well as other key components such as protein, carbohydrate, calcium, cholesterol, fibre and sodium. All the recipes in this collection are low in fat.

Above: Keep the food moving when cooking in a wok. Chopsticks like these can be used, or toss the food using two spatulas or wooden spoons.

Many contain less than five grams of total fat or less per serving, and a few are even lower in fat, with under one gram per serving. One or two classic recipes, such as Teriyaki Soba Noodles with Tofu or Swordfish with Citrus Dressing, contain slightly more fat, but even these contain less than the traditional versions.

For ease of reference, throughout the recipe section, all recipes with a single * after the recipe title contain a maximum of five grams of total fat, those with ** contain a maximum of 10 grams of total fat and those with *** contain up to 15 grams of total fat per portion. Each recipe also has a complete breakdown of the energy, protein, carbohydrate, cholesterol, calcium, fibre and sodium values of the food.

Although the recipes are low in fat, they lose nothing in terms of flavour. This practical cookbook will enable you to enjoy healthy Japanese and East Asian food with a clear conscience. All the recipes are easy to cook and many are so quick that you'll have supper on the table in less time than it would have taken to collect a takeaway.

Left: When food is cooked in a steamer, there is no need for any fat to be used. A bamboo steamer like this one is ideal. Several can be stacked on top of each other if needed.

THE LOW-FAT JAPANESE AND EAST ASIAN KITCHEN

Cooks in Japan and East Asia have much to teach us about low-fat cooking. Their traditional diet is largely composed of vegetables, with a healthy proportion of carbohydrate in the form of noodles or rice, protein in the form of tofu and only small amounts of meat or fish. Suggestions for using tofu and other ingredients specific to the region are given in this section, which also includes valuable advice about planning and maintaining a healthy low-fat diet.

HEALTHY EATING GUIDELINES

A healthy diet provides us with all the nutrients we need. By eating the right types, balance and proportions of foods, we are more likely to have more energy and a higher resistance to diseases and illnesses such as heart disease, cancers, bowel disorders and obesity.

By choosing a variety of foods every day, you are supplying your body with all the essential nutrients it needs. To get the balance right, it is important to know just how much of each type of food you should be eating.

Of the five main food groups, it is recommended that we eat at least five portions of fruit and vegetables a day, not including potatoes; carbohydrate foods such as noodles, cereals, rice and potatoes; moderate amounts of fish, poultry and dairy products; and small amounts of foods containing fat or sugar. A dish like Chicken and Mushroom Doniburi fits the prescription perfectly, with its balance of rice, lean chicken, mushrooms and spring onions (scallions).

THE ROLE OF FAT IN THE DIET

Fats shouldn't be cut out of our diets completely, as they are a valuable source of energy and make foods more palatable. However, lowering the fats, especially saturated fats, in your diet, may help you to lose weight, as well as reducing your risk of developing diseases.

Aim to limit your daily intake of fats to no more than 30–35 per cent of the total number of calories you consume. Each gram of fat provides nine calories, so a person eating 2,000 calories a day should not eat more than 70g/2¾oz of fat. Saturated fat should not comprise more than 10 per cent of the total calorie intake.

TYPES OF FAT

All fats in our foods are made up of building blocks of fatty acids and glycerol, and their properties vary according to each combination.

The two main types of fat are saturated and unsaturated. The unsaturated group is divided into

two further categories – polyunsaturated and monounsaturated fats. There is usually a combination of these types of unsaturated fat in foods that contain fat, but the amount of each type varies from one kind of food to another.

SATURATED FATS

These fats are usually hard at room temperature. They are not essential in the diet, and should be limited, as they are implicated in raising the level of cholesterol in the blood, which can increase the likelihood of heart disease.

The main sources of saturated fats are animal products, such as fatty cuts of meat and meat products; spreading fats that are solid at room temperature, such as butter, lard and margarine; and full-fat dairy products such as cream and cheese. Aside from meat, these ingredients are seldom found in Japanese and East Asian recipes, but it is also important to avoid coconut and palm oil, which are saturated fats of

Above: Tofu, which is also known as bean curd, is a highly nutritious vegetable protein. It is cholesterol-free and low in fat.

Above: Green, leafy vegetables, such as pak choi (bok choy), are delicious eaten raw in salads or stir-fried with just a drop of oil and some flavourings.

Above: Oily fish like salmon are a good source of the Omega-3 fatty acids that are good for our hearts. Very fresh fish can be eaten raw in sushi or sashimi.

vegetable origin. More insidious are those fats which, when processed, change the nature of the fat from unsaturated fatty acids to saturated ones. These are called "hydrogenated" fats, and should be strictly limited, so look out for that term on food labels.

Saturated fats are also found in many processed foods, such as chips (French fries) and savoury snacks, as well as cookies, pastries and cakes.

POLYUNSATURATED FATS

Small amounts of polyunsaturated fats are essential for good health, as they provide energy, can help to reduce cholesterol levels and enable the absorption of the fat-soluble vitamins A and D. The body can't manufacture polyunsaturated fatty acids, so they must be obtained from food. There are two types: those of vegetable or plant origin, known as Omega-6, which are found in sunflower oil, soft margarine, nuts and seeds; and Omega-3 fatty acids, which come from oily fish such

Left: East Asian cuisine makes the most of a wide variety of fresh fruit and vegetables, carbohydrates such as rice and noodles, and a wealth of herbs, spices and other flavourings.

as tuna, salmon, herring, mackerel and sardines as well as walnuts, soya beans, wheatgerm and rapeseed (canola) oil.

MONOUNSATURATED FATS

The best known monounsaturated fat is olive oil. This is not used in Asian cooking, but another monounsaturated oil, groundnut (peanut) oil, is a popular choice. It is ideal for stir-frying and gives food a delicious flavour. Monounsaturated fatty acids are also found in nuts such as almonds, and oily fish. They are thought to have the beneficial effect of reducing blood cholesterol levels.

THE CHOLESTEROL QUESTION

Cholesterol is a fat-like substance that occurs naturally in the body, and which we also acquire from food. It has a vital role, since it is the material from which many essential hormones and vitamin D are made. Cholesterol is carried around the body, attached to proteins called high density lipoproteins (HDLs), low density lipoproteins (LDLs) and very low density lipoproteins (VLDLs or triglycerides).

Eating too much saturated fat encourages the body to make more cholesterol than it can use or can rid itself of. After food has been consumed, the LDLs carry the fat in the blood to

the cells where it is required. Any surplus should be excreted from the body, but if there are too many LDLs in the blood, some of the fat will be deposited on the walls of the arteries. This furring up gradually narrows the arteries and is one of the most common causes of heart attacks and strokes.

By way of contrast, HDLs appear to protect against heart disease. Whether high triglyceride levels are risk factors remains unknown.

CUTTING DOWN ON FATS AND SATURATED FATS IN THE DIET

It is relatively easy to cut down on obvious sources of fat in the diet, like butter, oils, margarine, cream, whole milk and full-fat cheese, but it is also important to know about and check consumption of "hidden" fats.

By educating yourself and being aware of which foods are high in fats, and by making simple changes, you can reduce the total fat content of your diet quite considerably. Choose low-fat alternatives when selecting items like milk, cheese and salad dressings. If you are hungry, fill up on very low-fat foods, such as fruits and vegetables, and foods that are high in carbohydrates, such as bread, potatoes, rice or noodles.

PLANNING A LOW-FAT DIET

Cutting down on fat on an everyday basis means that we need to keep a close eye on the fat content of everything that we eat. This section provides some general guidelines, which are applicable to all cuisines.

CUTTING DOWN ON FAT IN THE DIET

Most of us eat about 115g/4oz of fat every day. Yet just 10g/¼oz, about the amount in a single packet of crisps (US potato chips) or a thin slice of Cheddar cheese, is all that we actually need.

Current nutritional thinking is more lenient than this, however, and suggests an upper daily limit of about 70g/2¾oz total fat.

Using low-fat recipes helps to reduce the overall daily intake of fat, but there are also lots of other ways of reducing the fat in your diet. Just follow the "eat less, try instead" suggestions below to discover how easy it can be.

• Eat less butter, margarine, other spreading fats and cooking oils. Try instead reduced-fat spreads, low-fat spreads or fat-free spreads. Butter or hard margarine should first be softened at room temperature so that they can be

Above: Keep the fruit bowl stocked with fruit, including exotic varieties like lychees, and you'll always have a fat-free snack to hand.

spread thinly. Alternatively, use low-fat cream cheese or low-fat soft cheese for sandwiches and toast.

• Eat less full-fat dairy products such as whole milk, cream, butter, hard margarine, crème fraîche, whole-milk yogurts and hard cheese. Try instead semi-skimmed (low-fat) or skimmed milk, low-fat or reduced-fat milk products, such as low-fat yogurts and low-fat soft cheeses, reduced-fat hard cheeses such as Cheddar, and reduced-fat crème fraîche. Silken tofu can be used instead of cream in soups and sauces. It is a good source of calcium and an excellent protein food.

• Eat fewer fatty cuts of meat and high fat meat products, such as pâtés, burgers, pies and sausages. Try instead naturally low-fat meats such as skinless chicken and turkey, ostrich and venison. When cooking lamb, beef or pork, use only the leanest cuts. Always cut away any visible fat and skin from meat before cooking. Try substituting low-fat protein ingredients like dried beans, lentils or tofu for some or all of the meat in a recipe.

• Eat more fish. It is easy to cook, tastes great, and if you use a steamer, you won't need to add any extra fat at all.

• Eat fewer hard cooking fats, such as lard or hard margarine. Try instead polyunsaturated or monounsaturated oils, such as sunflower or corn oil, and don't use too much.

• Eat fewer rich salad dressings and less full-fat mayonnaise. Try instead reduced-fat or fat-free dressings, or just a squeeze of lemon juice. Use a reduced-fat mayonnaise and thin it with puréed silken tofu for an even greater fat saving.

• Eat less fried food, especially deep-fried. Try fat-free cooking methods like steaming, grilling (broiling), baking or microwaving. Use non-stick pans with spray oil. When roasting or grilling meat, place it on a rack and drain off excess fat frequently.

Below: Sardines are a good source of unsaturated fat.

• Eat fewer deep-fried or sautéed potatoes. Boil or bake them instead, or use other carbohydrates. Avoid chow-mein noodles, which are high in fat.

• Cut down on oil when cooking. Choose heavy, good-quality non-stick pans and use spray oil for the lightest coverage. Moisten food with fat-free or low-fat liquids such as fruit juice, defatted stock, wine or even beer.

• Eat fewer high-fat snacks, such as chocolate, cookies, chips (French fries) and crisps. Try instead a piece of fruit, some vegetable crudités or some home-baked low-fat fruit cake.

Below: Choose lean cuts of meat and naturally low-fat meats such as skinless chicken and turkey.

FAT-FREE COOKING METHODS

Japanese and East Asian cooking uses a variety of low-fat and fat-free cooking methods, and by incorporating recipes from this region into your daily diet it is easy to bring down your total fat consumption. Where possible, steam, microwave or grill (broil) foods, without adding extra fat. Alternatively, braise in a defatted stock, wine or fruit juice, or stir-fry with just the merest amount of oil.

• By choosing a good quality, non-stick wok, such as the one above, you can keep the amount of fat needed for cooking foods to the absolute minimum. When cooking meat in a regular pan, dry-fry the meat to brown it, then tip it into a sieve and drain off the excess fat before returning it to the pan and adding the other ingredients. If you do need a little fat for cooking, choose an oil high in unsaturates, such as groundnut (peanut), sunflower or corn oil, or a spray oil.

• Eat less meat and more vegetables and noodles or other forms of pasta. A good method for making a small amount of meat such as beef steak go a long way is to place it in the freezer for 30 minutes and then slice it very thinly with a sharp knife. Meat prepared this way will cook very quickly with very little fat.

• When baking chicken or fish, wrap it in a loose package of foil or baking parchment, with a little wine or fruit juice. Add some fresh herbs or spices before sealing the parcel, if you like.

• It is often unnecessary to add fat when grilling (broiling) food. If the food shows signs of drying, lightly brush it with a small amount of unsaturated oil, such as sunflower, corn or olive oil. Microwaved foods seldom need the addition of fat, so add herbs or spices for extra flavour and colour.

• Steaming is the ideal way of cooking fish. If you like, arrange the fish on a bed of aromatic flavourings such as lemon or lime slices and sprigs of herbs. Alternatively, place finely shredded vegetables or seaweed in the base of the steamer to give the fish extra flavour.

• If you do not own a steamer, cook vegetables in a covered pan over low heat with just a little water, so that they cook in their own juices.
• Vegetables can be braised in the oven in low-fat or fat-free stock, wine or a little water with some chopped fresh or dried herbs.
• Try poaching foods such as chicken, fish or fruit in low-fat or fat-free stock or fruit juice.
• Plain rice or noodles make a very good low-fat accompaniment to most Japanese and East Asian dishes.

• The classic Asian technique of adding moisture and flavour to chicken by marinating it in a mixture of soy sauce and rice wine, with a little sesame oil, can be used with other meats too. You can also use a mixture of alcohol, herbs and spices, or vinegar or fruit juice. The marinade will also help to tenderize the meat and any remaining marinade can be used to baste the food while it is cooking.
• When serving vegetables, resist the temptation to add a knob or pat of butter. Instead, sprinkle with chopped fresh herbs.

LOW-FAT SPREADS IN COOKING

There is a huge variety of low-fat and reduced-fat spreads available at our supermarkets, along with some spreads that are very low in fat. Generally speaking, any very low-fat spreads with a fat content of around 20 per cent or less have a high water content. These are unsuitable for cooking and can only be used for spreading.

VEGETABLES

Naturally low in fat and bursting with vitamins and minerals, vegetables are one food group that should ideally make up the bulk of our daily diet. In Japan and East Asia cooks use vegetables freely in stir-fries and braised dishes, and have evolved a wide range of delicious vegetarian main courses to make the most of the abundant choice of vegetables on sale in markets.

In recent years an increasing number of exotic vegetables and fruits have been introduced to the West, and many Japanese varieties are now available, which makes Japanese cooking easier. It is interesting to see how Japanese and Western varieties of many ordinary vegetables, such as cucumber and pepper, differ in size, shape and taste.

AUBERGINES

Popular throughout East Asia, aubergines (eggplants) come in a variety of shapes, sizes and colours. They have a smoky, slightly bitter taste and spongy flesh that readily absorbs other flavours and oils. To avoid the absorption of too much fat, cut the aubergine into slices, and dry-fry these in a wok over medium heat for 4–5 minutes. They can also be braised, stuffed or baked.

BAMBOO SHOOTS

Fresh bamboo shoots are quite hard to buy outside Asia, but you may find them in big-city Asian markets. They must be parboiled before being cooked, as the raw vegetable contains a highly toxic oil. Remove the base and the hard

Above: There are numerous varieties of aubergines available.

outer leaves, then cut the core into chunks. Boil these in salted water for 30 minutes, then drain, rinse under cold water and drain again. Cut into slices, shreds or cubes for further cooking. Dried bamboo slices must be soaked in water for 2–3 hours before use. Canned bamboo shoots only need rinsing before being used.

BEANSPROUTS

Mung beans and soy beans are the varieties of beansprout most often used, and they are an important ingredient in the Asian kitchen. It is important to use them as fresh as possible. Better still, sprout the beans yourself. Before use, rinse them to remove the husks and tiny roots. Use them in salads or stir-fries, but take care not to overcook them.

CHINESE LEAVES

Also known as Chinese cabbage or Napa cabbage, this vegetable has pale green, crinkly leaves with long, wide, white ribs. It is crunchy, has a sweet, nutty flavour and tastes wonderful raw or cooked. When buying, look for firm, slightly heavy heads with pale green leaves without blemishes. To prepare, peel off the outer leaves, cut off the root and slice the cabbage thinly or thickly. When stir-fried, Chinese leaves lose their subtle cabbage taste and take on the flavour of other ingredients in the dish.

DAIKON

Also known as mooli, this Asian vegetable looks rather like a parsnip, but is actually related to the radish. The flavour is milder than that of most radishes, however, although the texture is similar: crisp and crunchy. Treat it like a carrot, scraping or peeling the outer skin and then slicing it in rounds or batons. Daikon can be eaten both raw or cooked.

KABOCHA

This vegetable plays an essential part in Japanese cooking. Originally from Central America, this Japanese squash has a dark green and ragged skin and is much smaller than Western squash varieties. The dense flesh is a rich yellow colour and, when boiled, becomes sweet and fluffy. Although it is highly calorific, kabocha is regarded as a health food for its nutritional content, containing both carotene and vitamin A. It has a mild chestnut aroma, and the flavour is also similar to, but not as sweet as, the chestnut. It is best simply steamed or boiled. It is also used for frying in tempura, as well as for simmering with other vegetables and chicken.

MUSHROOMS

Several types of mushrooms are used in Asian cooking, and many of these are now readily available in Asian stores and Western supermarkets.

Below: Daikon has a crisp, crunchy texture and is delicious raw.

Right: Pak choi tastes similar to spinach.

Above: Kabocha has a green skin and the flesh ranges from yellow to orange.

Straw mushrooms are small, grey-brown mushrooms that are grown on beds of rice straw, hence the name. They have an almost neutral flavour and are ideal for adding to stir-fries, braised dishes and soups. Fresh ones are not readily available in the West, but dried or canned ones can be found in Asian stores. They have a silky surface with a subtle, sweet taste and a slippery texture. Rinse canned ones before use, and take care not to overcook them.

Fresh shiitake mushrooms have a slightly acidic taste and a slippery texture. They contain twice as much protein as button mushrooms. To prepare, remove the stems, then either leave the caps whole or slice them.

Chinese mushrooms are the dried form of shiitake mushrooms. They have a dusky aroma and a fragrant flavour, which is intensified by the drying process. They are very versatile, but they must be reconstituted before being used. Soak them in a bowl of cold water overnight, or in a bowl or warm water for at least 30 minutes before using, then strain the soaking liquid and remove the stems.

Oyster mushrooms have a mild flavour and are pastel-coloured in shades of pink, yellow or pearl grey. They need gentle handling as they are very fragile. Tear, rather than cut, large specimens and don't overcook them, or they will become rubbery.

Cloud ear (wood ear) mushrooms are thin, brittle dried mushrooms, with a slippery yet crisp texture. They can be used in stir-fries, braises and soups. The fungus expands to six or eight times its volume after soaking, so use plenty of water in a large bowl. As a guide, a piece of fungus that would fit in a tablespoon would require at least 250ml/8fl oz/1 cup water. Cover the bowl and leave the fungus to soak for 30 minutes, then drain, rinse well and drain again. Discard any hard and sandy bits, then separate the larger clumps into individual "ears".

PAK CHOI

Another member of the brassica family, pak choi (bok choy) has lots of noms-de-plume, including horse's ear, Chinese cabbage and Chinese white cabbage. Unlike Chinese leaves, pak choi doesn't keep well, so plan to use it within a day or two of purchase. The vegetable is generally cooked, although very young and tender pak choi can be eaten raw. The stems need slightly longer cooking than the leaves.

SEAWEED

If you've never sampled seaweed before, it is a good idea to start with arame. Dried arame must be soaked in lukewarm water for 20 minutes before being used in salads or stir-fries, but it can be added straight from the packet to braised dishes or soups.

Konbu is a large seaweed, often called kelp. It is generally available dried, and must be reconstituted in cold water for 45 minutes before use. Don't wash off the powdery covering before soaking it; just wipe with a damp cloth. It is a rich source of vitamins and minerals, especially iodine.

Nori is wafer-thin dried seaweed, sold in sheets to be used as a wrapping for *sushi*. Grill (broil) the sheets briefly on one side for *sushi*, or on both sides for crumbling as a topping.

Wakame and Hijiki are similar forms of seaweed. Wakame is available fresh, and both are available dried, mostly pre-shredded. To prepare dried varieties, soak in warm water for 15 minutes until it softens and turns green, then drain it, blanch it in boiling water for 1 minute, drain again and refresh under cold water. Use as directed in the recipe.

WATER CHESTNUTS

Fresh, crisp water chestnuts are the corms of a plant that grows on the margins of rivers and lakes. They have snow-white flesh which stays crunchy even after long cooking. Fresh water chestnuts are often available from Asian markets. They keep well in a paper bag in the refrigerator. Once released from their dark brown jackets, however, they must be kept submerged in water in a covered container and used within one week. Canned water chestnuts should be rinsed thoroughly before being used as directed in the recipe.

Above: Dried and cut wakame, at front.

FRUIT

When embarking on a low-fat eating plan, it is all too easy to concentrate solely on the fat content of foods while ignoring the amount of sugar they contain. The occasional indulgence does no harm, but you should avoid following a sensible main course with a sugary dessert. Instead, end a meal with a piece of fresh fruit.

FIGS

These oval or pear-shaped fruits are among the most luscious of all and can be eaten fresh or dried. They are not juicy in the conventional sense, nor do they have a particularly strong flavour, but they are succulent and sweet.

Figs come in three main varieties – white, black and red – and range in colour from palest green to dark gold, burnished brown or deep purple. The entire fig is edible (although some people prefer to peel them), from the soft thin skin to the sweet succulent red or purplish flesh and the myriad tiny seeds. Skin colour makes little difference to the taste of a fig. Their high natural sugar content makes them the sweetest of all fruits. The flavour varies, depending on where they were grown and how ripe they are.

Ripe figs are very delicate and do not travel well, so it is often difficult to find imported fruit at a perfect stage of maturity. Look for unblemished fruit that is soft and yielding when gently squeezed but still holds its shape. Figs should have a faint, delicate aroma; if they smell sour, they are over-ripe and

Below: Limes can be used to make zesty dips.

Above: It is easy to obtain mango chunks if you score the flesh before slicing it off.

will taste sour too. If you are buying figs in their country of origin, you may find some with split skins. Provided you are going to eat them immediately, this does not matter. Be careful not to squash the figs on the way home, or you will end up with a squishy, inedible pulp.

KIWIS

These cylindrical fruit, 7.5–10cm/3–4in in length, are covered with a light brown fuzzy skin, which looks very dull in comparison with the beautiful bright green interior, with its crown of tiny edible black seeds arranged around a white core. The flavour is delicate, yet refreshing and tangy. Kiwi fruit were formerly known as Chinese gooseberries, in recognition of the fact that they originated in the Yangtze Valley.

Choose plump, unwrinkled fruit with unblemished skins. Kiwis are ripe when they yield to gentle pressure like a ripe pear; however, hard, unripe fruit can easily be ripened at home. Store at room temperature, but not in a bowl with other fruits, since the enzymes in kiwi fruit cause them to ripen very quickly. The skin of a kiwi fruit is edible, but the fuzzy texture is not particularly pleasant, so it is best to peel the fruit with a small sharp knife.

LIMES

Limes are the smallest members of the true citrus family. They have thin, fairly smooth, green skins and a highly aromatic, acid flavour. Unlike lemons, limes will grow in tropical regions. Limes are the most perishable of all citrus fruit and quickly dry out and develop brown patches on their skins. Choose

Above: Slices of star fruit not only taste delicious, but they look attractive too.

unblemished fruits that feel heavy for their size and avoid those with yellowish skins, as they may have lost some of their tanginess. Store limes in the fridge for up to a week. Limes can be used in the same way as lemons, but will add a sharper flavour, so use fewer of them. A few drops of lime juice squeezed over tropical fruit, such as papayas, melons and prickly pears will do wonders for the flavour.

MANGOES

There are many types of mango. Most are oval in shape with blushed gold or pink skin, although there are also green, scarlet and orange varieties. All are highly scented, with meltingly soft flesh that is invariably sweet and juicy. When buying mangoes, choose fruit with smooth, unblemished skin. If mango chunks are required for a recipe, the easiest way to obtain these is to cut a thick lengthways slice off either side of the unpeeled fruit. Score the flesh on each slice with criss-cross lines, cutting down to the skin. Fold these slices inside out and then slice off the flesh, which will be neatly cubed. Cut the remaining flesh off the stone.

STAR FRUIT

The correct name for this fruit is carambola. Cylindrical in shape, the bright yellow waxy-looking fruit has five distinctive "wings" or protuberances which form the points of the star shapes revealed when the fruit is sliced. The flavour varies: fruits that have been picked straight from the tree in Asia are inevitably sweet and scented, but those that have travelled long distances in cold storage can be disappointing.

FLAVOURINGS

The principal flavourings favoured in East Asia have made a tremendous contribution to global cuisine. Soy sauce is now a commonplace condiment and often finds its way into dishes that have no more than a nodding acquaintance with Japan or East Asia.

DASHI STOCK

Dashi is a fish stock made from water, konbu and dried skipjack tuna. It can be made at home, or you can buy freeze-dried granules called *dashi-no-moto* for an instant stock, if you prefer.

GINGER

Valued not just as an aromatic, but also for its medicinal qualities, ginger is used throughout Asia. Although commonly referred to as a root, ginger is actually a rhizome, or underground stem. When young, it is juicy and tender, with a sharp flavour suggestive of citrus. At this stage it can easily be sliced, chopped or pounded to a paste. Older roots are tougher and may need to be peeled and grated. Pickled ginger is delicious, and the Japanese type has a delicate flavour.

MIRIN

This amber-coloured, heavily sweetened sake is made from distilled sake. It is only used in cooking, and adds a mild sweetness, a slight alcoholic flavour and a shiny glaze to food. It is used for simmered dishes and in glazing sauces.

Below: Clockwise from top left, aka-miso, shiro-miso, hatcho-miso and kuro-miso.

MISO

Although lifestyles are rapidly changing, for many Japanese the day still starts with a bowl of miso soup for breakfast. Boiled *daizu* (soya beans) is crushed, then mixed with a culture called *koji*, which is made with wheat and rice, barley or beans. The fermented mixture is allowed to mature for up to three years. Numerous kinds and brands of miso are available in supermarkets, even outside Japan. They are categorized into three basic grades according to strength of flavour and colour: *shiro-miso* (white, light and made with rice), *aka-miso* (red, medium and made with barley), and *kuro-miso* (black, strong and made with soya beans).

Miso is quite salty and has a strong fermented bean flavour. *Shiro-miso* is the lightest in saltiness and flavour, *aka-miso* is of medium flavour, and the strongest is *kuro-miso*. *Hatcho-miso*, the best *kuro-miso* (black), is rich and salty, and is good for dipping sauces and soups. It is often used mixed with another lighter miso. There are less salty brands for the health conscious. Miso is a versatile ingredient and can be simply diluted with dashi stock to make soups, used as seasoning for simmered dishes or dipping sauces, and also as a marinade for meat and fish. If miso is overcooked it loses its subtle aroma, so add the paste towards the end of the cooking time. In soups, use sparingly.

Above: Light and dark shoyu.

RICE VINEGAR

Unlike *shoyu* and *miso*, Japanese vinegar is delicate tasting and good for adding subtle flavours to Japanese cooking. It is made from rice and, unless labelled *yonezu* (pure rice vinegar), most Japanese vinegars, called *su* or *kokumotsu-su*, normally contain other grains besides rice. If less than 40g/1½oz rice was used to make 1 litre/1¾ pint/4 cups of vinegar, it is labelled as *kokumotsu-su* (grain vinegar). There is also a cheap, mixed product, *gohsei-su*, which consists of brewed (about 60 per cent) and synthetic vinegar. Japanese rice vinegar has a mild, sweet aroma and has a less sharp taste than ordinary wine vinegar. The mild, acidic flavour disappears quickly, so add to hot dishes at the last minute.

SHOYU

Without doubt the single most important ingredient in Japanese cuisine, shoyu is used in almost every recipe. It is often used as a dip on its own for *sushi*, *sashimi*, pickles and many other dishes. Shoyu is quite salty, although less salty now than it used to be, due to recent warnings about the role of salty food in heart disease. There are basically two types: *usukuchi* (light), and *koikuchi*, (dark). The *usukuchi* is an all-purpose shoyu, clearer but slightly saltier than *koikuchi*, which is used for making sauces such as taré for *teriyaki*. There are also many grades, depending on the grade of soya beans, which are priced accordingly. *Tamari* is made from soya beans only without wheat, so it is similar to the liquid obtained during the making of miso.

RICE AND NOODLES

These low-fat, high-carbohydrate foods are immensely important in Japan and East Asia, forming the bulk of most meals. People in the north of China favour noodles, while those in the south prefer rice. Japanese and Korean cooks make excellent use of both.

RICE

Many Asians eat rice three times a day. It is the essential element of the meal and anything served with it is merely relish. Rice is a non-allergenic food, rich in complex carbohydrates and low in salts and fats. It contains small amounts of easily digestible protein, together with phosphorous, magnesium, potassium and zinc. Brown rice, which retains the bran, yields vitamin E and some B-group vitamins, and is also a source of fibre.

There are thousands of varieties of rice. In Japan, two basic types of rice are eaten. The first is a plump, short grained variety called *uruchimai*. This is the rice used for *sushi*. The grains cling together when cooked, although not as cohesively as when the second type, Japanese glutinous rice, is cooked. Steaming is the recommended method for cooking glutinous rice, since this encourages the rice to cook through without collapsing into mush.

NOODLES

Second only to rice as a staple food, noodles are enjoyed all over Asia. Usually mixed with other ingredients such as vegetables or seafood, rather than being served as an accompaniment, noodles are eaten at all times of day and are a popular breakfast food. Asian noodles are made from flours from a wide range of sources, including wheat, rice, mung bean, buckwheat, seaweed and devil's tongue, which is a plant related to the arum lily. Some noodles are plain, others are enriched with egg. They are sold fresh and dried.

Wheat noodles are made from water, wheat flour and salt. Japanese wheat noodles, udon, come in different thicknesses, and are sold in bundles, held in place by a paper band. The thin white ones are called somen.

Above: Black and white glutinous rice.

Egg noodles, which are enriched wheat noodles, are are made in various thicknesses and may be fresh or dried, in coils or blocks. Japanese egg noodles are sold as ramen.

Cellophane noodles consist of very fine, clear strands. They are also known as mung bean noodles, transparent noodles, bean thread noodles or glass noodles. In Japan they are known as *harusame*. When cooked, they remain firm, and it is their texture, rather than their bland taste, that appeals.

Rice noodles come in various forms, from very thin strands called rice vermicelli to flattened sheets.

Buckwheat noodles are darker in colour than wheat varieties. They are popular in Korea and also in Japan, where they are called soba.

Left: Fresh udon noodles and bundles of dried udon noodles.

MEAT AND POULTRY

It is traditional in Japan and East Asia for the meat element in a dish to be a small percentage of the whole, with vegetables and noodles or rice making up the major portion. This is good news for anyone on a low-fat diet. The eating of meat was banned in Japan for many years, first due to Buddhism and later by the Shogunate for 300 years until 1868. It was only after World War II that meat, mainly beef, pork and chicken, became a part of the general diet. It is still only sparingly used; nearly always thinly sliced and cooked with vegetables, or minced (ground), none of which require much additional fat.

BEEF

In much of East Asia, the cow was for many centuries regarded solely as a beast of burden, thus too precious to be slaughtered for food. Today, however, thanks to the fast-food industry, beef consumption is on the increase all over East Asia, and even in Japan, which was for centuries a Buddhist (and therefore vegetarian) culture. There are four types of *wagyu*, (Japanese beef): black, reddish brown, hornless and short-horned. Black beef is the most common. *Matsuzaka* beef, also known as Kobe beef, *omi* beef and *yonezawa* beef, are the top-quality meats. They are fed with beer and massaged regularly, which helps to distribute the fat, so making the lean meat more tender, and *wagyu* meat is pink rather than red. Wagyu is not available in the West but you can use sirloin or fillet instead.

PORK

The leanest cut of pork is fillet (tenderloin). There's very little waste with this cut, and it is perfect for stir-frying. Since ancient times pork has been eaten in Japan, even during the period when meat was banned, and it remains popular today. It is thinly sliced, pan-fried and mixed with grated fresh root ginger and shoyu, or else chopped and used as a flavouring in vegetable dishes. Long-simmered pork is delicious with ramen.

POULTRY

Native regional chickens, called *jidori*, are popular in Japan, though there are also many mass-produced broiler chickens. *Nagoya kochin* is one such jidori, with a pinkish golden, firm meat. Minced (ground) chicken is often used for making meatballs, sauces or as a flavouring for simmered vegetables. *Yakitori* is chicken pieces threaded on a bamboo skewer, then grilled (broiled) with sweet taré sauce. Boneless chicken thighs marinated in *teriyaki* sauce are ideal for cooking on barbecues.

Much higher in saturated fat than chicken, especially if you eat the skin, duck is best kept for occasional treats, or used in small quantities in combination with lots of vegetables, such as in a dish like Duck with Pancakes.

LAMB

Although not as popular as pork or beef, lamb is nevertheless an important ingredient in some classic Asian dishes, particularly those that originated in Mongolia or Tibet, such as Mongolian Firepot. Because it is a fatty meat, remove any visible fat from the meat before cooking, and use only sparingly, padding out the meal with plenty of fresh vegetables or low-fat carbohydrates, such as rice.

Below: Clockwise from front left, soft or silken tofu, lightly seared tofu and regular, firmer tofu.

Above: Finely sliced beef for sukiyaki.

TOFU: AN ALTERNATIVE PROTEIN

Packed with vitamins, tofu is a gift to the health-conscious cook. An excellent source of vegetable protein, it contains the eight essential amino acids that cannot be synthesized in the body, plus vitamins A and B. It is also low in fat, cholesterol-free and easy to digest. Substituting tofu for meat in just a couple of meals a week is an easy way of reducing overall fat consumption.

Made from soya beans that have been boiled, mashed, sieved (strained) and curdled, tofu comes in various forms. The firm type, *momen-goshi* (cotton-sieved tofu) is sold in blocks and can be cubed or sliced for use in a stir-fry, as kebabs or in salads. *Kinu-goshi*, sold as silken tofu in the West, has a smooth texture, is ideal for sauces and dips, and is a useful non-dairy alternative to cream, soft cheese or yogurt. Smoked, marinated and deep-fried tofu, called *atsu-age* in Japan, are also available.

Of itself, tofu has little flavour, but its sponge-like texture means that it absorbs other flavours easily. Seasonings such as ginger, soy sauce, oyster sauce and fermented black beans go particularly well with tofu.

FISH AND SHELLFISH

Fish is an extremely important food source in Japan and East Asia, where coastal waters, rivers and lakes provide an abundant harvest. From a healthy eating perspective, bass and sea bass, cod, sea bream, sole and plaice are excellent low-fat protein foods, but the darker-fleshed oily fish like tuna, salmon, carp, trout, mackerel, sardines and herring excite even more interest. The Omega-3 fatty acids they contain benefit the heart, helping to lower cholesterol and triglyceride levels and reduce blood pressure. Scallops and squid are also a good source of Omega-3 fatty acids, and these, along with prawns (shrimp), crab and clams are used to great effect by Asian cooks, whether steamed, poached, baked or fried. In Japan, a country with one of the highest rates of fish consumption in the world, exceedingly fresh fish is frequently served raw as *sashimi* or *sushi*.

Above: Fresh salmon, a popular ingredient for sashimi, *and salmon caviar.*

SALMON

The finest wild salmon has a superb flavour and makes excellent *sashimi*. The king of salmon in Japan is chum salmon, which has a perfect silvery body. It comes back to the river of its birth for spawning from September to January in Japan and some are caught for artificial insemination to be later released. Ishikari, a region on Hokkaido, the northernmost island, is famous for its salmon fisheries.

Salmon is costly, however, and so you may not be affordable on a regular basis. Responsibly farmed salmon is more economical to buy, and although the flavour is not quite as good as that of wild salmon, it is still delicious. The rosy flesh is beautifully moist and responds very well to being poached or baked, either on its own or with herbs

Below: Swordfish is usually sold in blocks or steaks.

and spices or aromatics. Salmon can take quite robust flavours. Try it with sweet soy sauce and noodles, or in that classic dish, Salmon Teriyaki. If you are buying salmon to make sashimi, ask a good fishmonger cut you a chunk from a large salmon; do not use ready-cut steaks. Smoked salmon can be used for *sushi*.

SCALLOPS

The tender, sweet flesh of this seafood needs very little cooking. Whenever possible, buy scallops fresh. If they are to be used for *sashimi*, the coral (roe), black stomach and frill must be removed first. In cooked dishes, the coral can be retained and is regarded as a delicacy.

SHRIMPS AND PRAWNS

If you ask for shrimp in Britain, you will be given tiny crustaceans, while in America, the term is used for the larger shellfish which the British call prawns. Asian cooks use both words fairly indiscriminately, so check exactly what a recipe requires before buying. Choose raw shellfish if possible, and then cook it yourself. This applies equally to fresh and frozen mixed seafood. If frozen, thaw slowly and pat them dry before cooking.

Above: Raw, unshelled prawns

SQUID

The cardinal rule with squid is to either fry it very quickly, or cook it for a long time in dishes, as happens in dishes such as Simmered Squid with Daikon. Anything in between will result in seafood that is tough and rubbery.

SWORDFISH

Used throughout Asia, swordfish have a long sword-like beak and a big fin on the back. These fish inhabit subtropical to tropical seas and grow to 3–5m/10–16½ft, some weighing over 500kg/1,100lb. They have a taste and firm texture similar to tuna, and it has a light pink flesh. In Japan it is often used for processed foods but can also be eaten raw as *sashimi* or marinated and simply grilled (broiled) or lightly fried.

TUNA

This very large fish is usually sold as steaks, which can be pink or red, depending on the variety. Avoid tuna steaks with heavy discoloration around the bone, or which are brownish and dull-looking. The flesh should be solid and compact.

In Japan, tuna is normally displayed cut into thick rectangular pieces – convenient for *sashimi*. There are usually two kinds, *akami* and *toro*, depending on which part of the fish the flesh comes from. *Akami*, red meat, is from the main, upper part of the body and toro, oily meat, is from the lower. It is sometimes classified by the degree of oiliness into *chu-toro*, middle toro, or *o-toro*, big toro. *Akami* was more popular than toro before World War II, but now it is generally thought that *toro* is superior in taste to *akami* and it is thus priced accordingly.

Below: Tuna steaks and salmon cutlets

SASHIMI AND *SUSHI*

Glowing colours, exquisite presentation and pure, clean flavours are just some of the reasons why *sashimi* and *sushi* have become popular the world over. Both these Japanese specialities are generally, but not inevitably, based upon raw fish, which must be absolutely fresh and of the finest quality.

For *sashimi*, fish is shaved into paper-thin slices or cut into chunks or finger-width slices. It is traditionally served with wasabi, an extremely hot condiment made from a plant that grows near mountain streams.

Sushi is a general term relating to a variety of snacks or light dishes based on rice that has been prepared in a particular way. It frequently includes fish. The most familiar version, *hoso-maki*, involves laying the rice on a sheet of nori seaweed and rolling it around one or more ingredients before slicing it into rolls. The rice can also be compressed into blocks and topped with fresh or smoked fish (as pictured above), or shaped by hand and coated in sesame seeds to make *onigiri*.

FAT AND CALORIE CONTENTS OF FOOD

The figures show the weight of fat (g) and the energy content per 100g (3½oz) of each of the following foods used in Japanese and East Asian cooking. Use the table to help work out the fat content of favourite dishes.

	fat (g)	Energy kcals/kJ
MEATS		
Beef minced (ground), raw	16.2	225kcal/934kJ
Beef, rump (round) steak, lean only	4.1	125kcal/526kJ
Beef, fillet (tenderloin) steak	8.5	191kcal/799kJ
Chicken, minced (ground), raw	8.5	106kcal/449kJ
Chicken fillet, raw	1.1	106kcal/449kJ
Chicken thighs, without skin, raw	6.0	126kcal/530kJ
Duck, without skin, cooked	9.5	182kcal/765kJ
Lamb leg, lean, cooked	6.3	198kcal/831kJ
Liver, lamb's, raw	6.2	137kcal/575kJ
Pork, average, lean, raw	4.0	123kcal/519kJ
Pork, lean roast	4.0	163kcal/685kJ
Pork, minced (ground), raw	4.0	123kcal/519kJ
Pork, ribs, raw	10.0	114kcal/480kJ
Turkey, meat only, raw	1.6	105kcal/443kJ
Turkey, minced (ground), raw	6.5	170kcal/715kJ
FISH AND SHELLFISH		
Cod, raw	0.7	80kcal/337kJ
Crab meat, raw	0.5	54kcal/230kJ
Mackerel, raw	16.0	221kcal/930kJ
Monkfish, raw	1.5	76kcal/320kJ
Mussels, raw, weight without shells	1.8	74kcal/312kJ
Mussels, raw, weight with shells	0.6	24kcal/98kJ
Oysters, raw	4.2	120kcal/508kJ
Prawns (shrimp)	1.0	76kcal/320kJ
Salmon, steamed	13.0	200kcal/837kJ
Scallops, raw	1.6	105kcal/440kJ
Sardine fillets, grilled	10.4	195kcal/815kJ
Sardines, grilled, weight with bones	6.3	19kcal/497kJ
Sea bass, raw	2.0	97kcal/406kJ
Squid, boiled	1.0	79kcal/330kJ
Swordfish, grilled	5.1	155kcal/649kJ
Tuna, grilled	6.3	184kcal/770kJ

	fat (g)	Energy kcals/kJ
VEGETABLES		
Asparagus	0.0	12.5kcal/52.5kJ
Aubergine (eggplant)	0.4	15kcal/63kJ
Bamboo shoots	0.0	29kcal/120kJ
Beansprouts	1.6	10kcal/42kJ
(Bell) peppers	0.4	32kcals/128kJ
Beans, fine green	0.0	7kcal/29kJ
Beetroot (beets)	0.1	36kcal/151kJ
Broccoli	0.9	33kcal/138kJ
Carrot	0.3	35kcal/156kJ
Celery	0.2	7kcal/142kJ
Chilli, fresh	0.0	30kcal/120kJ
Chinese leaves (Chinese cabbage)	0.0	8kcal/35kJ
Courgettes (zucchini)	0.4	18kcal74kJ
Cucumber	0.1	10kcal/40kJ
Daikon (mooli)	0.1	18kcal74kJ
Fennel	0.0	12kcal/50kJ
Leek	0.3	20kcal/87kJ
Mangetouts (snow peas)	0.4	81kcal/339kJ
Mushrooms, button (white)	0.5	24kcal/100kJ
Mushrooms, shiitake	0.2	55kcal/230kJ
Mushrooms, dried Chinese	0.0	56kcal/240kJ
Onion	0.2	36kcal/151kJ
Pak choi (bok choy)	0.0	13kcal/53kJ
Spinach (fresh, cooked)	0.0	20kcal/87kJ
Spring onion (scallion)	0.0	17kcal/83kJ
Sweet potato (peeled, boiled)	0.0	84kcal/358kJ
Water chestnuts	0.0	98kcal/410kJ
NUTS AND SEEDS		
Almonds	55.8	612kcal/2534kJ
Cashew nuts	48.0	573kcal/2406kJ
Chestnuts	2.7	169kcal/714kJ
Sesame seeds	47.0	507kcal/2113kJ

Below: Red meats such as beef, lamb and pork have a higher quantity of fat per 100g than white meat.

Below: Seafood is a good source of vitamins, minerals and protein. Oily fish contains high levels of Omega-3 fatty acids.

FRUIT	fat (g)	Energy kcals/kJ
Apples, eating	0.1	47kcal/199kJ
Bananas	0.3	95kcal/403kJ
Grapefruit	0.1	30kcal/126kJ
Grapes (green)	0.0	56kcal/235kJ
Lychees	0.1	58kcal/248kJ
Mangoes	0.0	60Kcal/251kJ
Nectarine	0.0	40kcal/169kJ
Oranges	0.1	37kcal/158kJ
Peaches	0.0	31kcal/132kJ
Pears	0.1	40kcal/169kJ
Pineapple, fresh	0.0	50Kcal/209kJ
Pineapple, canned chunks	0.2	63Kcal/264kJ
Raspberries	0.0	28Kcal/117kJ
Star fruit (carambola)	0.0	25Kcal/105kJ
Strawberries	0.0	27kcal/113kJ
Watermelon	0.0	23kcal/95kJ

BEANS, CEREALS AND TOFU	fat (g)	Energy kcals/kJ
Aduki beans, cooked	0.2	123kcal/525kJ
Noodles, cellophane	trace	351kcal/1468kJ
Noodles, egg	0.5	62kcal/264kJ
Noodles, plain wheat	2.5	354kcal/1190kJ
Noodles, rice	0.1	360kcal/1506kJ
Noodles, soba	0.1	99kcal/414kJ
Rice, brown, uncooked	2.8	357kcal/1518kJ
Rice, white, uncooked	3.6	383kcal/1630kJ
Tofu, firm	4.2	73kcal/304kJ
Tofu, silken	2.5	55kcal/230kJ

BAKING AND PANTRY	fat (g)	Energy kcals/kJ
Cornflour (cornstarch)	0.7	354kcal/1508kJ
Flour, plain (all-purpose) white	1.3	341kcal/1450kJ
Flour, self-raising (self-rising)	1.2	330kcal/1407kJ
Flour, wholemeal (whole-wheat)	2.2	310kcal/1318kJ
Tapioca	0.0	28kcal/119kJ
Honey	0.0	288kcal/1229kJ
Soy sauce, per 5ml/1 tsp	0.0	9kcal/40kJ
Sugar, white	0.3	94kcal/1680kJ

FATS, OILS AND EGGS	fat (g)	Energy kcals/kJ
Butter	81.7	737kcal/3031kJ
Low-fat spread	40.5	390kcal/1605kJ
Very low-fat spread	25.0	273kcal/1128kJ
Oil, corn, per 15ml/1 tbsp	13.8	124kcal/511kJ
Oil, groundnut (peanut), per 15ml/1 tbsp	14.9	134kcal/552kJ
Oil, rapeseed (canola), per 15ml/1 tbsp	13.7	124kcal/511kJ
Oil, sesame seed, per 15ml/1 tbsp	14.9	134kcal/552kJ
Oil, sunflower, per 15ml/1 tbsp	13.8	124kcal/511kJ
Eggs	10.8	147kcal/612kJ
Egg yolk	30.5	339kcal/1402kJ
Egg white	Trace	36kcal/153kJ

DAIRY PRODUCTS	fat (g)	Energy kcals/kJ
Cheese, Cheddar	34.4	412kcal/1708kJ
Cheese, Cheddar-type, reduced fat	15.0	261kcal/1091kJ
Cheese, cottage	3.9	98kcal/413kJ
Cheese, cream	47.4	439kcal/1807kJ
Cream, double (heavy)	48.0	449kcal/1849kJ
Cream, reduced-fat double (heavy)	24.0	243kcal/1002kJ
Cream, single (light)	19.1	198kcal/817kJ
Cream, whipping	39.3	373kcal/1539kJ
Crème fraîche	40.0	379kcal/156kJ
Crème fraîche, reduced fat	15.0	165kcal/683kJ
Fromage frais, plain	7.1	113kcal/469kJ
Fromage frais, very low fat	0.2	58kcal/247kJ
Milk, full cream (whole)	3.9	66kcal/275kJ
Milk, semi-skimmed (low-fat)	1.5	35kcal/146kJ
Milk, skimmed	0.1	33kcal/130kJ
Yogurt, low-fat natural (plain)	0.8	56kcal/236kJ
Yogurt, Greek (US strained plain)	9.1	115kcal/477kJ

Below: Vegetables are very low in fat. Eat them raw for a filling snack, or steam them to retain maximum nutritional value.

Below: Soya products, such as tofu, soya milk and soya beans, contain isoflavones that are thought to lower cholesterol levels.

SOUPS AND APPETIZERS

These superb dishes are uniformly low in fat but hit the heights when it comes to flavour and presentation. Unusual soups such as Rice in Green Tea with Salmon or Miso Broth with Tofu make a marvellous opening to a special meal, and Grilled Vegetable Sticks are great with drinks. For something slightly more substantial, opt for Wakame with Prawns and Cucumber or Nori-rolled Sushi. The fresh, colourful ingredients and immaculate presentation will please the eye and the stomach.

MISO BROTH WITH TOFU ★

THE JAPANESE EAT MISO BROTH, A SIMPLE BUT HIGHLY NUTRITIOUS SOUP, ALMOST EVERY DAY — IT IS STANDARD BREAKFAST FARE AND IT IS ALSO EATEN WITH RICE OR NOODLES LATER IN THE DAY.

SERVES 4

INGREDIENTS

1 bunch of spring onions (scallions)
   or 5 baby leeks
15g/½ oz fresh coriander (cilantro),
   including the stalks
3 thin slices fresh root ginger
2 star anise
1 small dried red chilli
1.2 litres/2 pints/5 cups dashi stock
   or vegetable stock
225g/8oz pak choi (bok choy) or
   other Asian greens, thickly sliced
200g/7oz firm tofu, cut into
   2.5cm/1in cubes
60ml/4 tbsp red miso
30–45ml/2–3 tbsp shoyu
1 fresh red chilli, seeded and
   shredded (optional)

1 Cut the coarse green tops off the spring onions or baby leeks and slice the rest finely on the diagonal. Place the tops in a large pan.

2 Remove the coriander leaves from the stalks, and set the leaves aside. Add the coriander stalks, fresh root ginger, star anise and dried chilli to the pan. Pour in the dashi or vegetable stock.

3 Heat the mixture gently until it is boiling, then lower the heat and simmer for 10 minutes. Strain, return to the pan and reheat until simmering.

4 Add the green portion of the sliced spring onions or leeks to the soup with the pak choi or greens and tofu. Cook for 2 minutes.

5 Mix 45ml/3 tbsp of the miso with a little of the hot soup in a bowl, then stir it into the soup. Taste the soup and add more miso with soy sauce to taste.

6 Chop the reserved coriander leaves roughly and stir most of them into the soup with the white part of the spring onions or leeks.

7 Cook for 1 minute, then ladle the soup into warmed serving bowls. Sprinkle with the remaining coriander and the fresh red chilli, if using, and serve at once.

COOK'S TIP
• Dashi powder is available in most Asian and Chinese stores. Alternatively, make your own by gently simmering 10–15cm/4–6in konbu seaweed in 1.2 litres/2 pints/5 cups water for 10 minutes. Do not boil the stock vigorously as this makes the dashi bitter. Remove the konbu, then add 15g/½oz dried bonito flakes and bring to the boil. Strain immediately through a fine sieve.
• If you prefer not to use dashi stock, you can substitute instant or home-made vegetable stock in its place.

Energy 71Kcal/297kJ; Protein 7.2g; Carbohydrate 4.2g, of which sugars 3.5g; Fat 2.9g, of which saturates 0.4g; Cholesterol 0mg; Calcium 372mg; Fibre 2.6g; Sodium 884mg.

MISO SOUP WITH PORK AND VEGETABLES ★★

THIS IS QUITE A RICH AND FILLING SOUP. ITS JAPANESE NAME, TANUKI JIRU, MEANS RACCOON SOUP FOR HUNTERS, BUT AS RACCOONS ARE NOT EATEN NOWADAYS, IT IS BASED ON PORK.

SERVES 4

INGREDIENTS

- 200g/7oz lean boneless pork
- 15cm/6in piece *gobo* or 1 parsnip
- 50g/2oz daikon (mooli)
- 4 fresh shiitake mushrooms
- ½ *konnyaku* or 115g/4oz firm tofu
- 15ml/1 tbsp sesame oil, for stir-frying
- 600ml/1 pint/2½ cups instant dashi stock
- 70ml/4½ tbsp miso
- 2 spring onions (scallions), chopped
- 5ml/1 tsp sesame seeds

1 Slice the meat horizontally into very thin long strips, then cut the strips crossways into stamp-size pieces. Set the pork aside.

2 Peel the *gobo*, then cut it diagonally into 1cm/½in thick slices. Quickly plunge the slices into a bowl of cold water. If you are using parsnip, peel, cut it in half lengthways, then cut it into 1cm/½in thick half-moon-shaped slices.

3 Peel and slice the daikon into 1.5cm/⅔in thick discs. Shave the edge of the discs, then cut into 1.5cm/⅔in cubes.

4 Remove the shiitake stalks and cut the caps into quarters.

5 Cook the *konnyaku* in a pan of boiling water for 1 minute. Drain and cool. Cut in quarters lengthways, then crossways into 3mm/⅛in thick pieces.

6 Heat the sesame oil in a heavy pan. Stir-fry the pork, then add tofu, if using, *konnyaku* and all the vegetables except the spring onions. As soon as the colour of the meat changes, add the stock.

7 Bring to the boil over a medium heat. Keep skimming off the foam until the soup looks clear. Reduce the heat, cover, and simmer for 15 minutes.

8 Mix the miso with 60ml/4 tbsp hot stock to make a smooth paste. Stir one-third into the soup. Taste and add more if required. Add the spring onions and remove the pan from the heat. Serve hot in soup bowls and sprinkle with sesame seeds.

Energy 134Kcal/558kJ; Protein 14.4g; Carbohydrate 3.4g, of which sugars 1.9g; Fat 7.1g, of which saturates 1.4g; Cholesterol 32mg; Calcium 173mg; Fibre 1.4g; Sodium 308mg.

JAPANESE-STYLE NOODLE SOUP ★

THIS DELICATE, FRAGRANT SOUP IS FLAVOURED WITH JUST A HINT OF CHILLI. IT IS BEST SERVED AS A LIGHT LUNCH OR AS A FIRST COURSE. IT LOOKS VERY PRETTY WITH THE NOODLES AND VEGETABLES.

SERVES 4

INGREDIENTS

   45ml/3 tbsp *aka-miso*
   200g/7oz/scant 2 cups udon noodles,
     soba noodles or egg noodles
   30ml/2 tbsp sake or dry sherry
   15ml/1 tbsp rice or wine vinegar
   45ml/3 tbsp shoyu
   115g/4oz asparagus tips or
     mangetouts (snow peas), thinly
     sliced diagonally
   50g/2oz/scant 1 cup shiitake
     mushrooms, stalks removed and
     caps thinly sliced
   1 carrot, sliced into julienne strips
   3 spring onions (scallions), thinly
     sliced diagonally
salt and ground black pepper
5ml/1 tsp dried chilli flakes, to serve

COOK'S TIP

Miso is a thick fermented paste based on cooked soya beans with rice or a similar cereal. It adds a savoury flavour to dishes. There are various types, *aka-miso* being medium strength.

1 Bring 1 litre/1¾ pints/4 cups water to the boil in a pan. Pour 150ml/¼ pint/⅔ cup of the boiling water over the miso and stir until it has dissolved.

2 Meanwhile, bring another large pan of lightly salted water to the boil, add the noodles and cook according to the packet instructions until they are just tender.

3 Drain the noodles in a colander. Rinse under cold water, then drain again.

4 Thoroughly combine the sake or sherry, vinegar and soy sauce in a small bowl, then add to the pan of boiling water.

5 Boil the mixture gently for 3 minutes, then reduce the heat and stir in the miso mixture.

6 Add the asparagus or mangetouts, mushrooms, carrot and spring onions, and simmer for 2 minutes until the vegetables are just tender. Season.

7 Divide the noodles among four warm bowls and pour the soup over the top. Serve sprinkled with the chilli flakes.

Energy 223Kcal/942kJ; Protein 7.5g; Carbohydrate 40.9g, of which sugars 3.8g; Fat 3.4g, of which saturates 0.1g; Cholesterol 0mg; Calcium 29mg; Fibre 2.5g; Sodium 807mg.

RICE IN GREEN TEA WITH SALMON ★

ACCORDING TO A CHINESE PROVERB, IT IS BETTER TO BE DEPRIVED OF FOOD FOR THREE DAYS THAN TEA FOR ONE. THIS RECIPE ENABLES YOU TO HAVE BOTH, AND VERY DELICIOUS IT IS TOO.

SERVES 4

INGREDIENTS
150g/5oz salmon fillet
¼ sheet nori seaweed
250g/9oz/1¼ cups Japanese short
  grain rice cooked using 350ml/
  12fl oz/1½ cups water
15ml/1 tbsp *sencha* leaves
5ml/1 tsp wasabi paste (optional)
20ml/4 tsp shoyu
salt

1 Thoroughly salt the salmon fillet and leave for 30 minutes. If the salmon fillet is thicker than 2.5cm/1in, slice it in half and salt both halves.

2 Wipe the salt off the salmon with kitchen paper and grill (broil) the fish under a preheated grill (broiler) for about 5 minutes until cooked through. Remove the skin and any bones, then roughly flake the salmon with a fork.

3 Using scissors, cut the nori into short, narrow strips about 20 x 5mm/¾ x ¼in long, or leave as long narrow strips, if you prefer.

4 If the cooked rice is warm, put equal amounts into individual rice bowls or soup bowls.

5 If the rice is cold, put it in a sieve (strainer) and pour hot water from a kettle over it to warm it up. Drain, then spoon it into the bowls. Place the salmon pieces on top of the rice.

6 Put the *sencha* leaves in a teapot. Bring 600ml/1 pint/2½ cups water to the boil, remove from the heat and allow to cool slightly.

7 Pour into the teapot and wait for 45 seconds. Strain the tea gently and evenly over the top of the rice and salmon. Add some nori and wasabi, if using, to the top of the rice, then trickle shoyu over and serve.

COOK'S TIPS
The word "*sencha*" simply means "commonplace" or "ordinary" in Japanese, and *sencha* leaves are what the popular Japanese green tea is made from. They are often packaged simply as loose green tea leaves.

Energy 294Kcal/1229kJ; Protein 12.4g; Carbohydrate 50.3g, of which sugars 0.4g; Fat 4.5g, of which saturates 0.7g; Cholesterol 19mg; Calcium 21mg; Fibre 0g; Sodium 373mg.

GRILLED VEGETABLE STICKS ★★

FOR THIS TASTY DISH, MADE WITH TOFU, KONNYAKU AND AUBERGINE, YOU WILL NEED 40 BAMBOO SKEWERS, SOAKED IN WATER TO PREVENT THEM FROM BURNING WHILE BEING COOKED.

SERVES 4

INGREDIENTS
1 × 285g/10¼oz packet firm tofu
1 × 250g/9oz packet *konnyaku*
2 small aubergines (eggplants)
25ml/1½ tbsp toasted sesame oil
For the yellow and green sauces
45ml/3 tbsp *shiro-miso*
15ml/1 tbsp caster (superfine) sugar
5 young spinach leaves
2.5ml/½ tsp *sansho*
salt
For the red sauce
15ml/1 tbsp *aka-miso*
5ml/1 tsp caster (superfine) sugar
5ml/1 tsp mirin
To garnish
pinch of white poppy seeds
15ml/1 tbsp toasted sesame seeds

1 Drain the liquid from the tofu packet and wrap the tofu in three layers of kitchen paper.

2 Set a plate on top to press out the remaining liquid. Leave for 30 minutes until the excess liquid has been absorbed by the kitchen paper. Cut into eight 7.5 × 2 × 1cm/3 × ¾ × ½in slices.

3 Drain the liquid from the *konnyaku*. Cut it in half and put in a small pan with enough water to cover. Bring to the boil and cook for about 5 minutes. Drain and cut it into eight 6 × 2 × 1cm/ 2½ × ¾ × ½in slices.

4 Halve the aubergines lengthways, then halve the thickness to make four flat slices. Soak in cold water for 15 minutes. Drain and pat dry.

5 To make the yellow sauce, mix the *shiro-miso* and the sugar in a pan, then cook over a low heat, stirring to dissolve the sugar. Remove the pan from the heat. Place half the sauce in a small bowl.

6 Blanch the spinach leaves in rapidly boiling water with a pinch of salt for 30 seconds and drain, then cool under running water. Squeeze out as much of the water as possible and chop finely.

7 Transfer the chopped spinach to a mortar and pound to a paste using a pestle. Mix the paste and *sansho* pepper into the bowl of yellow sauce to make the green sauce.

8 Put all the red sauce ingredients in a small pan and cook over a low heat, stirring constantly, until the sugar has dissolved. Remove from the heat.

9 Pierce the slices of tofu, *konnyaku* and aubergine with two bamboo skewers each. Heat the grill (broiler) to high. Brush the aubergine slices with sesame oil and grill (broil) for 7–8 minutes each side. Turn several times.

10 Grill the konnyaku and tofu slices for 3–5 minutes each side, or until lightly browned. Remove them from the heat but keep the grill hot.

11 Spread the red miso sauce on the aubergine slices. Spread one side of the tofu slices with green sauce and one side of the *konnyaku* with the yellow miso sauce from the pan. Grill the slices for 1–2 minutes. Sprinkle the aubergines with poppy seeds. Sprinkle the *konnyaku* with sesame seeds and serve all together.

Energy 132Kcal/549kJ; Protein 11.8g; Carbohydrate 6.5g, of which sugars 5.8g; Fat 6.7g, of which saturates 0.9g; Cholesterol 0mg; Calcium 711mg; Fibre 1.3g; Sodium 291mg.

W A K A M E WITH P R A W N S AND C U C U M B E R ★

THIS SALAD-STYLE DISH, CALLED SUNO-MONO IN JAPAN, USES WAKAME SEAWEED, WHICH IS NOT ONLY RICH IN MINERALS, B COMPLEX VITAMINS AND VITAMIN C, BUT ALSO MAKES YOUR HAIR SHINY.

2 Peel the prawns, including the tails. Insert a cocktail stick (toothpick) into the back of each prawn and gently scoop up the thin black vein running down its length. Pull it out, then throw it away.

3 Add the prawns to a pan of lightly salted boiling water and cook until they curl up completely to make full circles. Drain and cool.

4 Halve the cucumber lengthways. Peel away half of the green skin with a zester or vegetable peeler to create green and white stripes. Scoop out the centre with a tablespoon. Slice the cucumber very thinly with a sharp knife or a mandolin. Sprinkle with 5ml/1 tsp salt, and leave for 15 minutes in a sieve (strainer), to draw out excess liquid.

5 Bring a large pan of water to the boil and blanch the wakame briefly. Drain and cool under cold running water. Add to the cucumber in the sieve.

6 Press the cucumber and wakame to remove the excess liquid. Repeat the rinsing, draining and pressing process two to three times.

7 Mix the dressing ingredients in a mixing bowl. Stir well until the sugar has dissolved. Add the wakame and cucumber to the dressing and mix.

8 Pile up the wakame mixture in four small bowls or on four plates. Prop the prawns against the heap. Garnish with ginger and serve immediately.

SERVES 4

INGREDIENTS
   10g/¼oz dried wakame seaweed
   12 medium raw tiger prawns
      (jumbo shrimp), heads removed
      but tails intact
   ½ cucumber
   salt
For the dressing
   60ml/4 tbsp rice vinegar
   15ml/1 tbsp shoyu
   7.5ml/1½ tsp caster
      (superfine) sugar
   2.5cm/1in fresh root ginger, peeled
      and cut into thin strips, to garnish

1 Soak the wakame in a pan or bowl of cold water for 15 minutes until fully open. The wakame expands to three to five times its original size. Drain.

VARIATION
For a vegetarian version, replace the shellfish with some toasted pine nuts.

Energy 37Kcal/154kJ; Protein 6.9g; Carbohydrate 1.7g, of which sugars 1.7g; Fat 0.3g, of which saturates 0g; Cholesterol 73mg; Calcium 35mg; Fibre 0.2g; Sodium 339mg.

SCALLOPS SASHIMI IN MUSTARD SAUCE ★

THANKS TO THEIR SUBTLE SWEETNESS AND APPEALING TEXTURE, SCALLOPS MAKE THE MOST SUPERB SUSHI. SERVE THIS LAUDABLY LOW-FAT DISH AS A SNACK OR WITH OTHER APPETIZERS.

SERVES 4

INGREDIENTS
    8 scallops or 16 queen scallops,
      cleaned and coral removed
    ¼ dried sheet chrysanthemum petals
      (sold as *kiku nori*) or a handful of
      edible flower petals such as
      yellow nasturtium
    leaves from 4 bunches of watercress
For the dressing
    30ml/2 tbsp shoyu
    5ml/1 tsp sake or dry sherry
    10ml/2 tsp English (hot) mustard

1 Slice the scallops in three horizontally then cut them in half crossways. If you use queen scallops, slice them in two horizontally.

2 Put the dried chrysanthemum or the flower petals in a sieve (strainer). Pour hot water from a kettle all over, and leave to drain for a while. When cool, gently squeeze the excess water out. Set aside and repeat with the watercress.

3 Mix together all the ingredients for the dressing in a bowl. Add the scallops 5 minutes before serving and mix well without breaking them.

4 Add the flower petals and the watercress, then transfer to four small bowls. Serve cold. Add a little more shoyu, if required.

COOK'S TIPS
• Substitute the watercress with the finely chopped green part of spring onions (scallions).
• Do not pick chrysanthemums from your garden, as the edible species are different to ornamental ones. Fresh edible flowers are now increasingly available at specialist Japanese stores, or look for dried ones in Asian stores.

Energy 73Kcal/311kJ; Protein 13.3g; Carbohydrate 2.5g, of which sugars 0.8g; Fat 1.2g, of which saturates 0.4g; Cholesterol 24mg; Calcium 101mg; Fibre 0.8g; Sodium 649mg.

NORI-ROLLED SUSHI ★

YOU WILL NEED A MAKISU (A SUSHI ROLLING MAT) TO MAKE THESE TWO TYPES OF SUSHI. THERE ARE TWO TYPES: HOSO-MAKI IS THIN-ROLLED SUSHI, WHILE FUTO-MAKI IS THE THICK-ROLLED TYPE.

SERVES 6–8

FUTO-MAKI (THICK-ROLLED SUSHI)
MAKES 16 PIECES

INGREDIENTS
For the vinegared rice
    200g/7oz/1 cup *sushi* rice soaked
       for 20 minutes in water to cover
    45ml/3 tbsp rice vinegar
    30ml/2 tbsp sugar
    5ml/1 tsp coarse salt
For the omelette
    2 eggs, beaten
    25ml/1½ tbsp water mixed with
       5ml/1 tsp dashi powder
    10ml/2 tsp sake
    2.5ml/½ tsp salt
    vegetable oil, for frying
For the fillings
    4 dried shiitake mushrooms, soaked
       in water for 30 minutes
    120ml/4fl oz/½ cup water mixed with
       7.5ml/1½ tsp dashi powder
    15ml/1 tbsp shoyu
    7.5ml/1½ tsp caster (superfine) sugar
    5ml/1 tsp mirin
    6 raw large prawns (shrimp), heads
       and shells removed, tails intact
    2 sheets nori seaweed
    4 asparagus spears, steamed for
       1 minute
    10 chives, about 23cm/9in long,
       ends trimmed

1 Drain the rice. Put it in a pan with 290ml/9fl oz/1⅓ cups water. Bring to the boil, then cover and simmer for about 15 minutes, or until all the water has been absorbed. Meanwhile, heat the vinegar, sugar and salt, stir well and cool. Add to the hot rice, then cover the pan and set aside for 20 minutes.

2 To make the omelette, mix the beaten eggs, dashi stock, sake and salt in a bowl. Heat a little oil in a frying pan on a medium-low heat. Pour in just enough egg mixture to thinly cover the base of the pan. As soon as the mixture sets, fold the omelette in half towards you and wipe the space left with a little oil.

3 With the first omelette still in the pan, repeat this process of frying and folding to make more omelettes. Each new one is laid on to the previous omelette, to form one multi-layered omelette. When all the mixture is used, slide the layered omelette on to a chopping board. Cool, then cut into 1cm/½in wide strips.

4 Put the shiitake mushrooms, dashi stock, shoyu, sugar and mirin in a small pan. Bring to the boil then reduce the heat. Cook for 20 minutes until half of the liquid has evaporated. Drain, remove the mushroom stems, and slice the caps thinly. Squeeze out any excess liquid, then dry on kitchen paper.

5 Make three cuts in the belly of each of the prawns to stop them curling up, and boil in salted water for 1 minute, or until they turn bright pink. Drain and cool, then remove the vein from each.

6 Place a nori sheet at the front edge of the *makisu*. Scoop up half of the rice and spread it on the nori sheet. Leave a 1cm/½in margin at the side nearest you, and 2cm/¾in at the side furthest from you.

7 Make a shallow depression horizontally across the centre of the rice. Fill this with a row of omelette strips, then put half the asparagus and prawns on top. Place five chives alongside, and then put half the shiitake slices on to the chives.

8 Lift the *makisu* with your thumbs while pressing the fillings with your fingers and roll up gently.

9 When completed, gently roll the *makisu* on the chopping board to firm it up. Unwrap and set the futo-maki aside. Repeat the process to make another roll.

HOSO-MAKI (THIN-ROLLED SUSHI)
MAKES 24 PIECES

INGREDIENTS
    2 sheets nori seaweed, cut in
       half crossways
    1 quantity vinegared rice
       (see recipe left)
    45ml/3 tbsp wasabi paste, plus
       extra for serving
For the fillings
    90g/3½oz very fresh tuna steak
    10cm/4in cucumber
    5ml/1 tsp roasted sesame seeds
    6cm/2½in *takuan* [daikon (mooli)
       pickle], cut into long strips
       1cm/½in thick

1 For the fillings, cut the tuna with the grain into 1cm/½in wide strips. Cut the cucumber into 1cm/½in thick strips.

2 Place the *makisu* on the work surface, then place a nori seaweed sheet on it horizontally, rough-side up. Spread a quarter of the vinegared rice over the nori to cover evenly, leaving a 1cm/½in margin on the side furthest from you. Press firmly to smooth the surface.

3 Spread a little wasabi paste across the rice and arrange some of the tuna strips horizontally in a row across the middle. Cut off any excess tuna which may be overhanging the edge of the rice.

Energy 71Kcal/296kJ; Protein 2.3g; Carbohydrate 12g, of which sugars 2.1g; Fat 1.5g, of which saturates 0.3g; Cholesterol 30mg; Calcium 10mg; Fibre 0g; Sodium 204mg.

4 Hold the *makisu* with both hands and carefully roll it up, wrapping the tuna in the middle, and rolling away from the side closest to you. Hold the rolled *makisu* with both hands and squeeze gently to firm the roll.

5 Slowly unwrap the *makisu*, remove the rolled tuna *hoso-maki* and set aside. Make another tuna *hoso-maki* with the remaining ingredients.

6 Repeat the same process using only the cucumber strips with the green skin on. Sprinkle sesame seeds on the cucumber before rolling.

7 Repeat with the *takuan* strips, but omit the wasabi paste. Keep the *sushi* on a slightly damp chopping board, covered with clear film (plastic wrap) during preparation. When finished, you should have two *hoso-maki* of tuna, and one each of cucumber and takuan.

To serve the *sushi*

1 Cut each *futo-maki* roll into eight pieces, using a very sharp knife. Wipe the knife with a dish towel dampened with rice vinegar after each cut. Cut each *hoso-maki* into six pieces in the same way.

2 Line up all the *maki* on a large tray. Serve with small dishes of wasabi, *gari* (pickled ginger) and shoyu for dipping.

COOK'S TIP
Half-fill a small bowl with water and add 30ml/2 tbsp rice vinegar. Use this to wet your hands to prevent the rice sticking when rolling *sushi*.

Energy 52Kcal/217kJ; Protein 2.1g; Carbohydrate 8g, of which sugars 1.4g; Fat 1.3g, of which saturates 0.2g; Cholesterol 17mg; Calcium 7mg; Fibre 0g; Sodium 90mg.

VEGETARIAN MAIN COURSES

Vegetarians are well catered for in Japan and East Asia, where tofu and fresh vegetables are key ingredients, along with carbohydrates such as rice and noodles. Recipes like Simmered Tofu with Vegetables and Toasted Noodles with Vegetables are excellent choices since they are both filling and very low in fat. Most are also very quick to make — ideal for a mid-week supper. You can also use a range of seasonal vegetables to add variety and tailor recipes to your personal preferences.

STIR-FRIED RICE AND VEGETABLES ★★

THE GINGER GIVES THIS MIXED RICE AND VEGETABLE DISH A WONDERFUL FLAVOUR. SERVE IT AS A VEGETARIAN MAIN COURSE FOR TWO OR AS AN UNUSUAL VEGETABLE ACCOMPANIMENT.

SERVES 2–4

INGREDIENTS

115g/4oz/generous ½ cup brown basmati rice, rinsed and drained
350ml/12fl oz/1½ cups vegetable stock
2.5cm/1in piece fresh root ginger
1 garlic clove, halved
5cm/2in piece pared lemon rind
115g/4oz/1½ cups shiitake mushrooms
15ml/1 tbsp vegetable oil
175g/6oz baby carrots, trimmed
225g/8oz baby courgettes (zucchini), halved
175–225g/6–8oz/about 1½ cups broccoli, broken into florets
6 spring onions (scallions), diagonally sliced
15ml/1 tbsp light soy sauce
10ml/2 tsp toasted sesame oil

1 Put the rice in a pan and pour in the vegetable stock.

2 Thinly slice the ginger and add it to the pan with the garlic and lemon rind. Slowly bring to the boil, then lower the heat, cover and cook very gently for 20–25 minutes until the rice is tender.

3 Discard the flavourings and keep the pan covered so that the rice stays warm.

4 Slice the mushrooms, discarding the stems. Heat the oil in a wok and stir-fry the carrots for 4–5 minutes until partially tender.

5 Add the mushrooms and courgettes, stir-fry for 2–3 minutes, then add the broccoli and spring onions and cook for 3 minutes more, by which time all the vegetables should be tender but should still retain a bit of "bite".

6 Add the cooked rice to the vegetables, and toss briefly over the heat to mix and heat through. Toss with the soy sauce and sesame oil. Spoon into a bowl and serve immediately.

COOK'S TIP
Keep fresh root ginger in the freezer. It can be sliced or grated and thaws very quickly.

Energy 190Kcal/792kJ; Protein 6.3g; Carbohydrate 29.1g, of which sugars 5.6g; Fat 5.4g, of which saturates 0.8g; Cholesterol 0mg; Calcium 63mg; Fibre 3.2g; Sodium 285mg.

TOASTED NOODLES WITH VEGETABLES ★

SLIGHTLY CRISP NOODLE CAKES TOPPED WITH VEGETABLES MAKE A SUPERB DISH, AND THE VERY GOOD NEWS FOR THE HEALTH-CONSCIOUS IS THAT THE AMOUNT OF SATURATED FAT IS NEGLIGIBLE.

SERVES 4

INGREDIENTS

175g/6oz dried egg vermicelli
15ml/1 tbsp vegetable oil
2 garlic cloves, finely chopped
115g/4oz/1 cup baby corn cobs
115g/4oz/1½ cups fresh shiitake
  mushrooms, halved
3 celery sticks, sliced
1 carrot, diagonally sliced
115g/4oz/1 cup mangetouts
  (snow peas)
75g/3oz/¾ cup sliced, drained,
  canned bamboo shoots
15ml/1 tbsp cornflour (cornstarch)
15ml/1 tbsp cold water
15ml/1 tbsp dark soy sauce
5ml/1 tsp caster sugar
300ml/½ pint/1¼ cups
  vegetable stock
salt and ground white pepper
spring onion curls, to garnish

1 Bring a pan of lightly salted water to the boil. Add the egg noodles and cook according to instructions on the packet until just tender.

2 Drain the noodles in a sieve (strainer), refresh under cold water, drain again, then dry thoroughly on kitchen paper.

3 Heat 2.5ml/½ tsp oil in a non-stick frying pan or wok. When it starts to smoke, spread half the noodles over the base. Fry for 2–3 minutes until lightly toasted. Carefully turn the noodles over (they stick together like a cake), fry the other side, then slide on to a heated serving plate.

4 Repeat with the remaining noodles to make two cakes. Keep hot.

5 Heat the remaining oil in the clean pan, then fry the garlic for a few seconds. Halve the corn cobs lengthways, add to the pan with the mushrooms, then stir-fry for 3 minutes, adding a little water, if needed, to prevent the mixture from burning.

6 Add the celery, carrot, mangetouts and bamboo shoots to the pan. Stir-fry for 2 minutes or until the vegetables are crisp-tender.

VARIATION

Sliced fennel tastes good in this stir-fry, either as an addition or instead of the sliced bamboo shoots.

7 Mix the cornflour to a paste with 15ml/1 tbsp cold water. Add to the pan with the soy sauce, sugar and stock. Cook, stirring, until the sauce thickens.

8 Season to taste. Divide the vegetable mixture between the noodle cakes, garnish with the spring onion curls. Each cake serves two people.

Energy 214Kcal/893kJ; Protein 7g; Carbohydrate 38.6g, of which sugars 3.5g; Fat 3.4g, of which saturates 0.4g; Cholesterol 0mg; Calcium 44mg; Fibre 2.4g; Sodium 353mg.

SIMMERED TOFU WITH VEGETABLES ★

A TYPICAL JAPANESE DINNER AT HOME GENERALLY CONSISTS OF A SOUP, THREE DIFFERENT DISHES AND A BOWL OF RICE. ONE OF THE THREE DISHES IS ALWAYS A SIMMERED ONE LIKE THIS MUSHROOM MIXTURE.

SERVES 4

INGREDIENTS
    4 dried shiitake mushrooms
    450g/1lb daikon (mooli)
    350g/12oz firm tofu
    115g/4oz/¾ cup green beans,
    5ml/1 tsp rice (any except for
      fragrant Thai or white basmati)
    115g/4oz carrot, peeled and cut
      into 1cm/½in thick slices
    300g/11oz baby potatoes, unpeeled
    750ml/1¼ pints/3 cups
      vegetable stock
    30ml/2 tbsp caster
      (superfine) sugar
    75ml/5 tbsp shoyu
    45ml/3 tbsp sake
    15ml/1 tbsp mirin

1 Put the dried shiitake in a bowl. Add 250ml/8fl oz/1 cup water and soak for 2 hours. Drain, discarding the liquid. Remove and discard the stems.

2 Peel the daikon and slice it into 1cm/½in discs. Shave the edge off the daikon discs to ensure they will cook evenly. Put the slices in cold water to prevent them from discolouring.

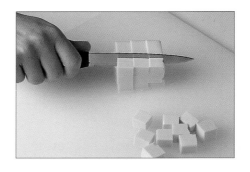

3 Drain and rinse the tofu, then pat dry with kitchen paper. Cut the tofu into pieces of about 2.5 × 5cm/1 × 2in.

4 Bring a pan of lightly salted water to the boil. Meanwhile, top and tail the beans, then cut them in half.

5 Blanch the beans in the boiling water for 2 minutes. Drain them in a sieve (strainer) and cool them under running water. Drain again.

6 Put the daikon slices in the clean pan. Pour in water to cover and add the rice. Bring to the boil, then reduce the heat and simmer for 15 minutes. Drain off the liquid and the rice.

7 Add the drained mushrooms, carrot and potatoes to the daikon in the pan.

8 Pour in the vegetable stock, bring the liquid to the boil, then reduce the heat to low and simmer.

9 Skim off any scum that comes to the surface of the liquid. Add the sugar, shoyu and sake and shake the pan gently to mix the ingredients thoroughly.

10 Cut a piece of baking parchment to a circle 1cm/½in smaller than the pan lid. Place the paper inside the pan, over the ingredients within.

11 Cover the pan with the lid and simmer for 30 minutes, or until the sauce has reduced by at least half.

12 Add the tofu and green beans and warm through for 2 minutes.

13 Remove the paper and add the mirin. Taste the sauce and adjust with shoyu if required. Serve immediately in warmed bowls.

COOK'S TIP
Once you have opened a packet of tofu, any that is unused should be rinsed and put in a bowl with fresh water to cover. Change the water every day and use the tofu within 5 days.

Energy 181Kcal/762kJ; Protein 10.3g; Carbohydrate 26.8g, of which sugars 14.8g; Fat 4.4g, of which saturates 0.7g; Cholesterol 0mg; Calcium 496mg; Fibre 3.1g; Sodium 833mg.

TERIYAKI SOBA NOODLES WITH TOFU ★★★

YOU CAN, OF COURSE, BUY READY-MADE TERIYAKI SAUCE, BUT IT IS EASY TO PREPARE AT HOME USING INGREDIENTS THAT ARE NOW READILY AVAILABLE IN SUPERMARKETS AND ASIAN SHOPS.

SERVES 4

INGREDIENTS
    350g/12oz soba noodles
    250g/9oz asparagus
    15ml/1 tbsp toasted sesame oil
    30ml/2 tbsp vegetable oil
    225g/8oz block firm tofu
    2 spring onions (scallions),
      cut diagonally
    1 carrot, cut into matchsticks
    2.5ml/½ tsp chilli flakes
    15ml/1 tbsp sesame seeds
    salt and ground black pepper
For the teriyaki sauce
    60ml/4 tbsp dark soy sauce
    60ml/4 tbsp sake or dry sherry
    60ml/4 tbsp mirin
    5ml/1 tsp caster
      (superfine) sugar

1 Cook the soba noodles according to the instructions on the packet, then drain and rinse under cold running water. Drain again and set aside.

2 Rinse the asparagus under cold running water, then trim using a sharp knife, and discard the woody ends. Cut into short lengths.

3 Lay the asparagus in a grill (broiler) pan, brush with sesame oil, then grill (broil) for 8–10 minutes, turning often, until they are tender. Set aside.

4 Meanwhile, heat the vegetable oil in a wok or large frying pan until it is very hot. Add the tofu to the pan and fry for 8–10 minutes until it is golden, turning it occasionally, using tongs or two wooden spoons, to crisp all sides.

5 Carefully remove the tofu from the wok or pan and leave to drain and cool slightly on kitchen paper. When is has cooled sufficiently, cut the tofu into 1cm/½in slices.

6 To make the teriyaki sauce, mix the soy sauce, sake or dry sherry, mirin and sugar together, then heat the mixture in the wok or frying pan.

7 Toss in the noodles and stir to coat in the sauce. Heat for 1–2 minutes, then spoon into warmed individual serving bowls with the tofu and asparagus. Sprinkle with the spring onions and carrot and sprinkle with the chilli flakes and sesame seeds. Serve immediately.

Energy 476Kcal/2007kJ; Protein 17g; Carbohydrate 71.6g, of which sugars 6.5g; Fat 13.7g, of which saturates 1g; Cholesterol 0mg; Calcium 332mg; Fibre 4.1g; Sodium 1081mg.

BRAISED TOFU WITH MUSHROOMS ★

THE SHIITAKE AND OYSTER MUSHROOMS FLAVOUR THE TOFU BEAUTIFULLY TO MAKE THIS THE PERFECT VEGETARIAN MAIN COURSE. IT CONTAINS VERY LITTLE SATURATED FAT.

SERVES 4

INGREDIENTS

350g/12oz tofu
2.5ml/½ tsp sesame oil
10ml/2 tsp light soy sauce
15ml/1 tbsp vegetable oil
2 garlic cloves, finely chopped
2.5ml/½ tsp grated fresh root ginger
115g/4oz/1 cup fresh shiitake
    mushrooms, stems removed
175g/6oz/2½ cups fresh
    oyster mushrooms
115g/4oz/1½ cups drained, canned
    straw mushrooms
115g/4oz/1½ cups button
    mushrooms, cut in half
15ml/1 tbsp dry sherry
15ml/1 tbsp dark soy sauce
90ml/6 tbsp vegetable stock
5ml/1 tsp cornflour (cornstarch)
15ml/1 tbsp cold water
salt and ground white pepper
2 spring onions (scallions), shredded

1 Put the tofu in a dish and sprinkle with the sesame oil, light soy sauce and a large pinch of pepper. Leave to marinate for 10 minutes, then drain. Use a sharp knife to cut the tofu into 2.5 x 1cm/1 x ½in pieces.

2 Heat the vegetable oil in a non-stick frying pan or wok. When it is very hot, fry the garlic and ginger for a few seconds. Add all the mushrooms and stir-fry for 2 minutes.

3 Stir in the sherry, soy sauce and stock, with salt, if needed, and pepper. Simmer for 4 minutes.

4 Mix the cornflour to a paste with the water. Stir into the pan or wok and cook, stirring, until thickened.

VARIATION
If fresh shiitake mushrooms are not available, use dried Chinese mushrooms soaked in hot water.

5 Carefully add the pieces of tofu, toss gently to coat thoroughly and simmer for 2 minutes.

6 Sprinkle the shredded spring onions over the top of the mixture, then transfer to a warm serving dish and serve immediately.

Energy 92Kcal/386kJ; Protein 9.6g; Carbohydrate 2.9g, of which sugars 1g; Fat 4.3g, of which saturates 0.6g; Cholesterol 0mg; Calcium 456mg; Fibre 1.4g; Sodium 456mg.

FISH AND SHELLFISH

Fish is an excellent source of protein, vitamins and minerals, has very little carbohydrate and contains oils that can have a positive impact on health. Some of our finest fish recipes come from Japan and East Asia, from sustaining Simmered Squid and Daikon to lightly cooked dishes like Steamed Red Snapper. Grills include the delicious Salmon Teriyaki and Marinated and Grilled Swordfish, and there are several delicious cold dishes to choose from too.

SIMMERED SQUID AND DAIKON ★

THE SECRET OF HOW TO MAKE THIS DISH USED TO BE HANDED DOWN FROM MOTHER TO DAUGHTER.
IT IS SERVED IN RESTAURANTS THESE DAYS BUT IS EASY TO MAKE AT HOME.

SERVES 4

INGREDIENTS

   450g/1lb squid, cleaned, body
     and tentacles separated
   900ml/1½ pints/3¾ cups water and
     5ml/1 tsp instant dashi powder
   about 1kg/2¼lb daikon
     (mooli), peeled
   60ml/4 tbsp shoyu
   45ml/3 tbsp sake or dry sherry
   15ml/1 tbsp caster (superfine) sugar
   30ml/2 tbsp mirin
   grated rind of ½ lime, to garnish

COOK'S TIP
When buying daikon look for one that is
at least 7.5cm/3in in diameter, with a
shiny, undamaged skin, and that sounds
dense and heavy when you pat it.

1 Separate the two triangular flaps from
the body of the squid, then cut the body
into 1cm/½in thick rings. Cut the
triangular flaps into 1cm/½in strips.

2 Cut off and discard 2.5cm/1in from
the thin end of the tentacles and chop
them into 4cm/1½in lengths. Make the
dashi stock.

3 Cut the daikon into 3cm/1¼in thick
rounds and shave off the edges with a
sharp knife. Plunge the slices into cold
water. Drain just before cooking.

4 Put the daikon and squid in a heavy
pan and pour on the stock. Bring to the
boil, and cook for 5 minutes, skimming
constantly. Reduce the heat and add the
shoyu, sake or sherry, sugar and mirin.

5 Cover the surface with a circle of
baking parchment cut 2.5cm/1in
smaller than the lid of the pan, and
simmer for 45 minutes, shaking the pan
occasionally. The liquid will reduce by
almost half.

6 Leave to stand for 5 minutes and
serve in small bowls with the lime rind.

Energy 153Kcal/643kJ; Protein 19.6g; Carbohydrate 11.8g, of which sugars 10.3g; Fat 2.4g, of which saturates 0.7g; Cholesterol 253mg; Calcium 67mg; Fibre 2.3g; Sodium 1221mg.

SALMON TERIYAKI ★★★

FOR THIS POPULAR DISH A SWEET SAUCE IS USED FOR MARINATING AS WELL AS FOR GLAZING THE FISH
AND VEGETABLES, GIVING THEM A SHINY GLOSS.

SERVES 4

INGREDIENTS

   4 small salmon fillets with skin,
     each weighing about 115g/4oz
   50g/2oz/¼ cup beansprouts, washed
   50g/2oz mangetouts (snow peas),
     ends trimmed
   20g/¾oz carrot, cut into
     thin strips
   salt
For the teriyaki sauce
   45ml/3 tbsp shoyu
   45ml/3 tbsp sake
   45ml/3 tbsp mirin
   15ml/1 tbsp plus 10ml/2 tsp
     caster (superfine) sugar

1 Mix all the ingredients for the teriyaki
sauce except for the 10ml/2 tsp sugar,
in a pan. Heat to dissolve the sugar.
Remove and cool for 1 hour.

2 Place the salmon fillets in a shallow
glass or china dish and pour over the
teriyaki sauce. Leave to marinate for
30 minutes.

3 Meanwhile, blanch the vegetables
in lightly salted water. First add the
beansprouts, then after 1 minute,
the mangetouts. Leave for 1 minute
again, and then add the thin carrot
strips. Remove the pan from the heat
after 1 minute, then drain the
vegetables and keep warm.

4 Preheat the grill (broiler) to medium.
Take the salmon fillet out of the sauce
and pat dry with kitchen paper. Reserve
the sauce.

5 Lightly oil a grill (broiling) pan. Grill
(broil) the salmon for 6 minutes, turning
once, until golden on both sides.

6 Pour the sauce into the pan. Add the
remaining sugar and heat until dissolved.
Remove from the heat. Brush the
salmon with the sauce, then grill until
the surface of the fish bubbles. Turn
over and repeat on the other side.

7 Heap the vegetables on to four heated
serving plates. Place the salmon on top
and spoon over the rest of the sauce.
Serve immediately.

Energy 239Kcal/995kJ; Protein 24.8g; Carbohydrate 2.1g, of which sugars 1.7g; Fat 13.3g, of which saturates 2.3g; Cholesterol 58mg; Calcium 93mg; Fibre 0.3g; Sodium 323mg.

VEGETABLES AND SALMON IN A PARCEL ★★★

IN THIS RECIPE, THE VEGETABLES AND SALMON ARE WRAPPED AND STEAMED WITH SAKE IN THEIR OWN MOISTURE. WHEN YOU OPEN THE PARCEL, YOU'LL FIND A COLOURFUL AUTUMN GARDEN INSIDE.

4 Slice the carrot very thinly, then with a Japanese vegetable cutter or sharp knife, cut out 8–12 maple-leaf or flower shapes. Carefully slice the spring onions in half lengthways with a sharp knife. Trim the mangetouts.

5 Cut four sheets of foil, each about 29 × 21cm/11½ × 8½in wide. Place the long side of one sheet facing towards you. Arrange the salmon and *shimeji* mushrooms in the centre, then place a spring onion diagonally across them. Put two shiitake on top, three to four mangetouts in a fan shape and then sprinkle with a few carrot leaves.

SERVES 4

INGREDIENTS
  450g/1lb salmon fillet, skinned
  30ml/2 tbsp sake or dry sherry
  15ml/1 tbsp shoyu, plus extra to
    serve (optional)
  about 250g/9oz/3 cups fresh
    shimeji mushrooms
  8 fresh shiitake mushrooms
  2.5cm/1in carrot
  2 spring onions (scallions)
  115g/4oz mangetouts (snow peas)
  salt

1 Cut the salmon into bitesize pieces. Marinate in the sake and shoyu for about 15 minutes, then drain and reserve the marinade. Preheat the oven to 190°C/375°F/Gas 5.

2 Clean the *shimeji* mushrooms and chop off the hard root. Remove and discard the stems from the shiitake.

3 Carve a shallow slit on the top of each shiitake with a sharp knife inserted at a slant. Repeat from the other side to cut out a notch about 4cm/1½in long, then rotate the shiitake 90° and carefully carve another notch to make a small white cross in the brown top.

6 Sprinkle the marinade and a good pinch of salt over the top. Fold the two longer sides of the foil together, then fold the shorter sides to seal. Repeat to make four parcels.

7 Place the parcels on a baking sheet and bake for 15–20 minutes in the middle of the preheated oven. When the foil has expanded into a balloon, the dish is ready to serve. Serve the parcels unopened with a little extra shoyu, if required.

Energy 231Kcal/964kJ; Protein 25.2g; Carbohydrate 3.9g, of which sugars 3.3g; Fat 12.9g, of which saturates 2.2g; Cholesterol 56mg; Calcium 49mg; Fibre 2g; Sodium 328mg.

STEAMED RED SNAPPER ★

ORIGINALLY, THIS ELEGANT DISH FEATURED A WHOLE RED SNAPPER WRAPPED IN LAYERED JAPANESE HANDMADE PAPER SOAKED IN SAKE AND TIED WITH RIBBONS. THIS VERSION IS A LITTLE EASIER.

SERVES 4

INGREDIENTS

    4 small red snapper fillets, no
    greater than 18 × 6cm/7 × 2½in,
    or whole snapper, 20cm/8in long,
    gutted but with head, tail and
    fins intact
    1 lime
    8 asparagus spears, hard
    ends snapped off
    4 spring onions (scallions)
    60ml/4 tbsp sake
    5ml/1 tsp shoyu (optional)
    salt

1 Sprinkle the red snapper fillets with salt on both sides and leave in the refrigerator for 20 minutes.

2 Preheat the oven to 180°C/350°F/Gas 4. Cut the lime in half. Grate one half and thinly slice the other.

3 To make the parcels, lay baking parchment measuring 38 × 30cm/15 × 12in on a work surface. Use two pieces for extra strength. Fold up one-third of the paper and turn back 1cm/½in from one end to make a flap.

4 Fold 1cm/½in in from the other end to make another flap. Fold the top edge down to fold over the first flap. Interlock the two flaps to form a long rectangle.

VARIATION
You could use any firm fish you like, such as salmon, trout, tuna or swordfish, in place of the red snapper in this quick and easy recipe.

5 At each end, fold the top corners down diagonally, then fold the bottom corners up to meet the opposite folded edge to make a triangle. Press flat with your palm. Repeat the process to make four parcels.

6 Cut 2.5cm/1in from the tip of the asparagus, and slice in half lengthways. Slice the asparagus stems and spring onions diagonally into thin ovals. Par-boil the tips for 1 minute in a small pan of lightly salted water and drain. Set aside.

7 Open the paper parcels. Place the asparagus slices and the spring onions inside. Sprinkle with salt and place the fish on top. Add more salt and some sake, then sprinkle in the lime rind. Refold the parcels.

8 Pour hot water from a kettle into a deep roasting pan fitted with a wire rack to 1cm/½in below the rack. Place the parcels on the rack. Cook in the centre of the preheated oven for 20 minutes. Check that the fish is cooked by carefully unfolding a parcel from one triangular side. The fish should have changed from translucent to white.

9 Transfer the parcels on to individual plates. Unfold both triangular ends on the plate and lift open the middle a little. Insert a thin slice of lime and place two asparagus tips on top. Serve immediately, asking the guests to open their own parcels. Add a little shoyu, if you like.

Energy 112Kcal/471kJ; Protein 20.6g; Carbohydrate 1g, of which sugars 0.9g; Fat 1.5g, of which saturates 0.3g; Cholesterol 37mg; Calcium 52mg; Fibre 0.6g; Sodium 79mg.

MARINATED AND GRILLED SWORDFISH ★★

THERE'S A TENDENCY FOR SWORDFISH TO TASTE RATHER DRY, SO FOR THIS RECIPE IT IS MARINATED IN A MISO MIXTURE WHICH KEEPS IT SUCCULENT EVEN WHEN COOKED ON THE BARBECUE.

2 Mix the miso and sake, then spread half across the bottom of the cleaned dish. Cover with a sheet of muslin or cheesecloth the size of a dish towel, folded in half, then open the fold.

3 Place the swordfish, side by side, on top, and cover with the muslin. Spread the rest of the miso mixture on the muslin. Make sure the muslin is touching the fish. Marinate for 2 days in the coolest part of the refrigerator.

4 Preheat the grill (broiler) to medium. Oil the wire rack and grill (broil) the fish slowly for about 8 minutes on each side, turning every 2 minutes. If the steaks are thin, check them frequently to see if they are ready.

5 Mix the shoyu and sake in a bowl. Grill the asparagus for 2 minutes on each side, then dip into the mixture. Return to the grill for 2 minutes more on each side. Dip in the sauce again and set aside.

6 Serve the fish hot on four individual serving plates. Garnish with the drained, grilled asparagus.

SERVES 4

INGREDIENTS
   4 × 175g/6oz swordfish steaks
   2.5ml/½ tsp salt
   300g/11oz *shiro-miso*
   45ml/3 tbsp sake
For the asparagus
   25ml/1½ tbsp shoyu
   25ml/1½ tbsp sake or
      dry sherry
   8 asparagus spears, the hard ends
      snapped off, each spear cut
      into three

1 Place the swordfish in a shallow dish. Sprinkle evenly with the salt on both sides and leave for 2 hours. Drain and wipe the fish with kitchen paper.

Energy 203Kcal/851kJ; Protein 32g; Carbohydrate 0.7g, of which sugars 0.6g; Fat 7.3g, of which saturates 1.6g; Cholesterol 72mg; Calcium 12mg; Fibre 0.2g; Sodium 495mg.

SWORDFISH WITH CITRUS DRESSING ★★★

FOR THIS BEAUTIFULLY PRESENTED SALAD, FRESH FISH IS SEARED OR MARINATED AND SLICED THINLY, THEN SERVED WITH SALAD LEAVES AND VEGETABLES.

SERVES 4

INGREDIENTS
  75g/3oz daikon (mooli), peeled
  50g/2oz carrot, peeled
  1 cucumber
  10ml/2 tsp vegetable oil
  300g/11oz skinned fresh swordfish
    steak, cut against the grain
  2 cartons mustard and cress
    (fine curled cress)
  15ml/1 tbsp toasted sesame seeds
For the dressing
  105ml/7 tbsp shoyu
  105ml/7 tbsp water and 5ml/1 tsp
    instant dashi powder
  30ml/2 tbsp toasted sesame oil
  juice of ½ lime
  rind of ½ lime, shredded into
    thin strips

1 Make the vegetable garnishes first. Use a very sharp knife, mandoline or vegetable slicer with a julienne blade to make very thin (about 4cm/1½in long) strands of daikon, carrot and cucumber.

2 Soak the daikon and carrot in ice-cold water for 5 minutes, then drain well and keep in the refrigerator.

3 Mix together all the ingredients for the dressing and stir well, then chill.

4 Heat the oil in a small frying pan until smoking hot. Sear the fish for 30 seconds on all sides.

5 Plunge the fish into cold water to stop the cooking. Dry on kitchen paper and wipe off as much oil as possible.

6 Cut the swordfish steak in half lengthways before slicing it into 5mm/¼in thick pieces in the other direction, against the grain.

7 Arrange the fish slices into a ring on individual plates. Mix the vegetable strands, mustard and cress (fine curled cress) and sesame seeds.

8 Shape the vegetable strands into a sphere. Gently place it on the swordfish. Pour the dressing around the plate's edge and serve immediately.

COOK'S TIP
If you cannot locate mustard and cress or fine curled cress, serve on a pile of wild rocket (arugula) leaves. You could also add grapefruit segments.

Energy 182Kcal/758kJ; Protein 15.2g; Carbohydrate 2.4g, of which sugars 2.3g; Fat 12.5g, of which saturates 2g; Cholesterol 31mg; Calcium 63mg; Fibre 1.1g; Sodium 645mg.

TEPPAN YAKI ★★

THIS IS NOT JUST A RECIPE, IT IS MORE OF AN EXPERIENCE. A FEAST OF FLAVOURS GIVES EVERY GUEST THE CHANCE TO GRILL HIS OR HER OWN FOOD AND DIP IT INTO ANY OF THE SAUCES PROVIDED.

SERVES 4

INGREDIENTS

275g/10oz monkfish tail
4 large scallops, cleaned and
  corals separated
250g/9oz squid body, cleaned
  and skinned
12 raw king or tiger prawns
  (jumbo shrimp), shells and heads
  removed, tails intact
115g/4oz/½ cup beansprouts, washed
1 red (bell) pepper, seeded and cut
  into 2.5cm/1in wide strips
8 fresh shiitake mushrooms,
  stems removed
1 red onion, cut into 5mm/¼in
  thick rounds
1 courgette (zucchini), cut into
  1cm/½in thick rounds
3 garlic cloves, thinly
  sliced lengthways
15ml/1 tbsp vegetable oil,
  for frying

Sauce A, radish and chilli sauce
8 radishes, finely grated
1 dried chilli, seeded and crushed
15ml/1 tbsp toasted sesame oil
½ onion, finely chopped
90ml/6 tbsp shoyu
30ml/2 tbsp caster
  (superfine) sugar
15ml/1 tbsp toasted
  sesame seeds
juice of ½ orange or 30ml/2 tbsp
  unsweetened orange juice

Sauce B, wasabi mayonnaise
60ml/4 tbsp reduced-fat mayonnaise
15ml/1 tbsp wasabi paste
5ml/1 tsp shoyu

Sauce C, lime and soy sauce
juice of 1 lime
grated rind and juice of 1 lime
20ml/4 tsp sake
90ml/6 tbsp shoyu
1 bunch chives, finely chopped

1 Sauce A In a small bowl, mix the grated radish, with its juice and with the chilli until it is thoroughly combined. Heat the sesame oil in a frying pan and fry the onion until soft.

2 Pour in the shoyu and add the sugar and sesame seeds, removing the pan from the heat just as it starts to boil.

3 Tip the mixture over the radish into the bowl and add the orange juice. Stir well and leave to cool.

4 Sauce B and C Mix the ingredients separately in small bowls, cover with clear film (plastic wrap) and set aside.

5 Cut the monkfish tail into 5mm/¼in slices. Halve the scallops horizontally.

6 With a small sharp knife, make neat shallow criss-cross slits in the skinned side of the squid. Slice into 2.5 × 4cm/1 × 1½in pieces.

7 Place all the seafood on half of a serving platter, and arrange all the prepared vegetables (apart from the garlic) on the other half. Divide sauces A and C among eight small dishes; these are for dipping. Put the wasabi mayonnaise in a small bowl with a teaspoon. Prepare serving plates as well.

8 Heat the griddle at the table and lightly oil it with a brush or kitchen paper. First, fry the garlic slices until crisp and golden. Remove the garlic chips to a small dish to mix with any sauces you like.

9 Guests cook ingredients on the griddle and either dip them into the sauces or eat them with the wasabi mayonnaise.

LEMON SOLE AND FRESH OYSTER SALAD ★★★

OYSTERS, WITH A RICE-VINEGAR DRESSING, TASTE WONDERFUL WITH LEMON SOLE SASHIMI. THIS SALAD IS A TYPICAL EXAMPLE OF HOW A JAPANESE CHEF WOULD PRESENT THE CATCH OF THE DAY.

SERVES 4

INGREDIENTS

1 very fresh lemon sole, skinned and
   filleted into 4 pieces
105ml/7 tbsp rice vinegar
dashi-konbu (dried kelp for stock), in 4
   pieces, big enough to cover the fillets
50g/2oz Japanese cucumber, ends
   trimmed, or ordinary salad
   cucumber with seeds removed
50g/2oz celery sticks,
   strings removed
450g/1lb large broad (fava)
   beans, podded
1 lime, ½ thinly sliced
60ml/4 tbsp walnut oil
seeds from ½ pomegranate
salt

For the oysters
15ml/1 tbsp rice vinegar
30ml/2 tbsp shoyu
15ml/1 tbsp sake or dry sherry
12 large fresh oysters, opened
25g/1oz daikon (mooli), peeled
   and very finely grated
8 chives

1 Sprinkle salt on the sole fillets. Cover and cool in the refrigerator for 1 hour.

2 Mix the rice vinegar and a similar amount of water in a bowl. Wash the fish fillets in the mixture, then drain well. Cut each fillet in half lengthways.

3 Lay one piece of *dashi-konbu* on a work surface. Place a pair of sole fillets, skinned sides together, on to it, then lay another piece of *konbu* on top. Cover all the fillets like this and chill for 3 hours.

4 Halve the cucumber crossways and slice thinly lengthways. Then slice again diagonally into 2cm/¾in wide pieces. Do the same for the celery. Sprinkle the cucumber with salt and leave to soften for 30–60 minutes. Gently squeeze to remove the moisture. Rinse if it tastes too salty, but drain well.

5 Boil the broad beans in lightly salted water for 15 minutes, or until soft. Drain and cool under running water, then peel off the skins to reveal the bright green beans inside. Sprinkle with salt.

6 Mix the rice vinegar, shoyu and sake for the oysters in a small bowl.

7 Slice the sole very thinly with a sharp knife. Remove the slightly chewy *dashi-konbu* first, if you prefer.

8 Place pieces of cucumber and celery in a small mound in the centre of four serving plates, then lay lime slices on top. Garnish with some chopped chives.

9 Place the oysters to one side of the cucumber, topped with a few broad beans, then season with 5ml/1 tsp of the vinegar mix and 10ml/2 tsp grated daikon. Arrange the sole *sashimi* on the other side and drizzle walnut oil and lime juice on top. Add pomegranate seeds and serve.

Energy 248Kcal/1036kJ; Protein 20g; Carbohydrate 14.1g, of which sugars 1.9g; Fat 12.7g, of which saturates 1.3g; Cholesterol 41mg; Calcium 108mg; Fibre 7.6g; Sodium 167mg.

CHICKEN AND DUCK

Poultry is popular in East Asia and Japan. In China, where thrift is highly prized, cooks tend to buy whole birds, whereas in Japan it is the breast fillets that are preferred. From a low-fat perspective, chicken is a more sensible choice than duck. Remove the skin and any obvious fat and use a low-fat cooking method like steaming, stir-frying or cooking in vegetable stock. Chicken with Mixed Vegetables and Kabocha Squash with Chicken Sauce are excellent options.

CHICKEN WITH MIXED VEGETABLES ★

EAST ASIAN COOKS ARE EXPERTS IN MAKING DELICIOUS DISHES FROM A RELATIVELY SMALL AMOUNT OF MEAT AND A LOT OF VEGETABLES. GOOD NEWS FOR ANYONE TRYING TO EAT LESS FAT.

2 Bring the stock to the boil in a pan. Add the chicken fillets and cook for 12 minutes, or until tender. Drain and slice, reserving 75ml/5 tbsp of the chicken stock.

3 Heat the remaining oil in a non-stick frying pan or wok, add all the vegetables and stir-fry for 2 minutes. Stir in the sherry, oyster sauce, caster sugar and reserved stock. Add the chicken to the pan and cook for 2 minutes more.

SERVES 4

INGREDIENTS
- 350g/12oz skinless chicken breast fillets
- 20ml/4 tsp vegetable oil
- 300ml/½ pint/1¼ cups chicken stock
- 75g/3oz/¾ cup drained, canned straw mushrooms
- 50g/2oz/½ cup sliced, drained, canned bamboo shoots
- 50g/2oz/⅓ cup drained, canned water chestnuts, sliced
- 1 small carrot, sliced
- 50g/2oz/½ cup mangetouts (snow peas)
- 15ml/1 tbsp dry sherry
- 15ml/1 tbsp oyster sauce
- 5ml/1 tsp caster (superfine) sugar
- 5ml/1 tsp cornflour (cornstarch)
- 15ml/1 tbsp cold water
- salt and ground white pepper

1 Put the chicken in a shallow bowl. Add 5ml/1 tsp of the oil, 1.5ml/¼ tsp salt and a pinch of pepper. Cover and set aside for 10 minutes in a cool place.

COOK'S TIP
Water chestnuts give a dish great texture as they remain crunchy, no matter how long you cook them for.

4 Mix the cornflour to a paste with the water. Add the mixture to the pan and cook, stirring, until the sauce thickens slightly. Season to taste with salt and pepper and serve immediately.

Energy 154Kcal/646kJ; Protein 22.2g; Carbohydrate 4.9g, of which sugars 3.4g; Fat 4.3g, of which saturates 0.7g; Cholesterol 61mg; Calcium 17mg; Fibre 1g; Sodium 61mg.

CHICKEN AND MUSHROOM DONBURI ★★

"DONBURI" IS A JAPANESE WORD, MEANING A ONE-DISH MEAL. THIS IS A SIMPLE VERSION, MIXING RICE AND SHIITAKE MUSHROOMS WITH PROTEIN IN THE FORM OF CHICKEN AND TOFU.

SERVES 4

INGREDIENTS

225–275g/8–10oz/generous
  1–1½ cups Japanese rice or
  Thai fragrant rice
30ml/2 tbsp vegetable oil
2 garlic cloves, crushed
2.5cm/1in piece fresh root
  ginger, grated
5 spring onions (scallions),
  diagonally sliced
1 fresh green chilli, seeded and
  finely sliced
3 skinless chicken breast fillets,
  cut into thin strips
150g/5oz tofu, cut into small cubes
115g/4oz/1¾ shiitake mushrooms,
  stems discarded and cups sliced
15ml/1 tbsp sake or dry sherry
30ml/2 tbsp light soy sauce
10ml/2 tsp granulated sugar
400ml/14fl oz/1⅔ cups chicken stock

4 Transfer the chicken mixture to a plate using a slotted spoon, and add the tofu to the pan.

5 Stir-fry the tofu for a few minutes, then add the mushrooms. Stir-fry for 2–3 minutes over medium heat until the mushrooms are tender.

6 Stir in the sake or sherry, soy sauce and sugar and cook the mixture briskly for 1–2 minutes, stirring all the time.

7 Return the chicken to the pan, toss over the heat for about 2 minutes, then pour in the stock. Stir well and cook over a gentle heat for 5–6 minutes until the sauce is bubbling.

8 Spoon the cooked rice into individual serving bowls and pile the chicken mixture on top, making sure that each portion gets a generous amount of chicken sauce.

1 Cook the rice in salted boiling water following the instructions on the packet.

2 While the rice is cooking, heat the oil in a large frying pan. Stir-fry the garlic, ginger, spring onions and chilli for 1–2 minutes until slightly softened.

3 Add the strips of chicken and fry, in batches if necessary, until all the pieces are evenly browned.

COOK'S TIP

Once the rice is cooked, leave it covered until you are ready to serve. It will stay warm for about 30 minutes. Fork through lightly to fluff up just before serving.

Energy 408Kcal/1709kJ; Protein 35.2g; Carbohydrate 46.3g, of which sugars 1.1g; Fat 8.8g, of which saturates 1.2g; Cholesterol 79mg; Calcium 216mg; Fibre 0.5g; Sodium 605mg.

CUBED CHICKEN AND VEGETABLES ★

A POPULAR JAPANESE COOKING STYLE SIMMERS VEGETABLES OF DIFFERENT TEXTURES WITH A SMALL AMOUNT OF MEAT TOGETHER IN DASHI STOCK. THIS CHICKEN VERSION IS KNOWN AS IRIDORI.

SERVES 4

INGREDIENTS
    2 skinless chicken thighs, about
      200g/7oz, boned
    1 large carrot, trimmed
    1 *konnyaku*
    300g/11oz *satoimo* or small potatoes
    500g/1¼lb canned bamboo shoots
    30ml/2 tbsp vegetable oil
    300ml/½ pint/1¼ cups water and
      7.5ml/1½ tsp instant dashi powder
    salt
For the simmering seasonings
    75ml/5 tbsp shoyu
    30ml/2 tbsp sake or dry sherry
    30ml/2 tbsp caster (superfine) sugar
    30ml/2 tbsp mirin

1 Cut the chicken into bitesize pieces. Chop the carrot into 2cm/¾in triangular chunks by cutting it diagonally and turning it 90 degrees each time you cut.

2 Boil the *konnyaku* in rapidly boiling water for 1 minute, then drain in a sieve (strainer) under running water. Cool, then slice it crossways into 5mm/¼in thick rectangular strips.

3 Cut a 4cm/1½in slit down the centre of a strip of cooled *konnyaku* without cutting the ends. Carefully push the top of the strip through the slit to make a decorative tie. Repeat with all of the *konnyaku* strips.

4 Peel and halve the *satoimo* or the new potatoes, if using. Put the pieces in a colander and sprinkle with a generous amount of salt. Rub well and wash under running water. Drain.

5 Drain and halve the canned bamboo shoots, then cut them into the same shape as the carrot.

6 In a medium pan, heat the vegetable oil and stir-fry the chicken pieces until the surface of the meat turns white.

7 Add the carrot, *konnyaku* ties, *satoimo* or potato and bamboo shoots. Stir well to thoroughly combine each time you add a new ingredient.

8 Add the dashi stock and bring to the boil. Cook on a high heat for 3 minutes then reduce to medium-low.

9 Add the shoyu, sake, sugar and mirin, cover the pan, then simmer for 15 minutes, until most of the liquid has evaporated, shaking the pan from time to time.

10 When the *satoimo* or potato is soft, remove the pan from the heat and spoon the chicken and vegetables into a large serving bowl. Serve immediately.

COOK'S TIP
When you cut *satoimo*, it produces a sticky juice. Rinsing with salt and water is the best way of washing it off the surface of the *satoimo*, your hands and any other surfaces it may have come into contact with.

Energy 101Kcal/430kJ; Protein 8.4g; Carbohydrate 16.1g, of which sugars 4.8g; Fat 0.8g, of which saturates 0.2g; Cholesterol 18mg; Calcium 65mg; Fibre 2.7g; Sodium 906mg.

KABOCHA SQUASH WITH CHICKEN SAUCE ★

IN THIS LOW-FAT DISH, THE MILD SWEETNESS OF KABOCHA SQUASH, WHICH TASTES RATHER LIKE SWEET POTATO, GOES VERY WELL WITH THE CHICKEN AND SAKE SAUCE.

SERVES 4

INGREDIENTS
   1 kabocha squash, about 500g/1¼lb
   ½ lime
   20g/¾oz mangetouts (snow peas)
   salt
For the chicken sauce
   100ml/3½fl oz/scant ½ cup water
   30ml/2 tbsp sake or dry sherry
   300g/11oz lean chicken,
    minced (ground)
   60ml/4 tbsp caster (superfine) sugar
   60ml/4 tbsp shoyu
   60ml/4 tbsp mirin

1 Halve the kabocha, then remove the seeds and fibre around the seeds. Halve again to make four wedges. Trim the stem end of each kabocha wedge.

2 Partially peel each wedge, cutting off two strips lengthways about 1–2.5cm/ ½–1in wide. The kabocha wedges will now have green (skin) and yellow (flesh) stripes. This will help preserve the kabocha's most tasty part just beneath the skin, and also allows it to be cooked until soft as well as being decorative.

3 Chop each wedge into large bitesize pieces. Place them side by side in a pan. Pour in enough water to cover, then sprinkle with some salt. Cover and cook for 5 minutes over a medium heat, then lower the heat and simmer for 15 minutes until tender.

4 Test the kabocha by pricking with a skewer. When soft enough, remove from the heat, cover and leave for 5 minutes.

5 Slice the lime into thin discs, then hollow out the inside of the skin to make rings of peel. Cover with a sheet of clear film (plastic wrap) until needed. Blanch the mangetouts in lightly salted water. Drain and set aside.

6 To make the chicken sauce, bring the water and sake to the boil in a pan. Add the chicken, and when the colour of the meat has changed, add the sugar, shoyu and mirin. Whisk together until the liquid has almost all evaporated.

7 Pile up the kabocha on a large plate, then pour the hot meat sauce on top. Add the mangetouts and serve, garnished with lime rings.

VARIATION
Use tofu for a vegetarian sauce. Wrap in kitchen paper and leave for 30 minutes. Mash with a fork, then add instead of the chicken in step 6.

Energy 165Kcal/701kJ; Protein 19.2g; Carbohydrate 18.8g, of which sugars 18.1g; Fat 1.1g, of which saturates 0.4g; Cholesterol 53mg; Calcium 51mg; Fibre 1.4g; Sodium 47mg.

DUCK WITH PANCAKES ★★

THIS HAS CONSIDERABLY LESS FAT THAN TRADITIONAL PEKING DUCK, BUT IS JUST AS DELICIOUS.
GUESTS SPREAD THEIR PANCAKES WITH SAUCE, ADD DUCK AND VEGETABLES, THEN ROLL THEM UP.

SERVES 4

INGREDIENTS
  15ml/1 tbsp clear honey
  1.5ml/¼ tsp five-spice powder
  1 garlic clove, finely chopped
  15ml/1 tbsp hoisin sauce
  2.5ml/½ tsp salt
  a large pinch of ground white pepper
  2 small skinless duck breast fillets
  ½ cucumber
  10 spring onions (scallions)
  3 leaves from a head of Chinese
    leaves (Chinese cabbage)
  12 Chinese pancakes (see Cook's Tip)
For the sauce
  5ml/1 tsp vegetable oil
  2 garlic cloves, chopped
  2 spring onions (scallions), chopped
  1cm/½in fresh root ginger, bruised
  60ml/4 tbsp hoisin sauce
  15ml/1 tbsp dry sherry
  15ml/1 tbsp cold water
  2.5ml/½ tsp sesame oil

1 Mix the honey, five-spice powder, garlic, hoisin sauce, salt and pepper in a shallow dish which is large enough to hold the duck fillets side by side. Add the duck fillets, and turn to coat them in the marinade.

2 Cover the dish with clear film (plastic wrap) and leave in a cool place to marinate for 2 hours, or overnight if you have the time.

3 Cut the cucumber in half lengthways. Using a teaspoon scrape out and discard the seeds. Cut the flesh into thin batons 5cm/2in long.

4 Cut off and discard the green tops from the spring onions. Finely shred the white parts and place on a serving plate with the cucumber batons.

5 Make the sauce. Heat the oil in a small pan and fry the garlic gently for a few seconds without browning. Add the spring onions, ginger, hoisin sauce, sherry and water. Cook gently for 5 minutes, stirring often, then strain and mix with the sesame oil.

6 Remove the duck fillets from the marinade and drain. Grill (broil) under a medium heat for 8–10 minutes on each side. Leave to cool for 5 minutes before cutting into thin slices. Arrange on a serving platter, cover and keep warm.

7 Line a bamboo steamer with the Chinese leaves and place the pancakes on top.

8 Pour boiling water into a large pan, to a depth of 5cm/2in. Cover the steamer and place it on a trivet in the pan of boiling water.

9 Steam for 2 minutes or until the pancakes are hot. Serve at once with the duck, cucumber, spring onions and the sauce.

COOK'S TIP
Chinese pancakes can be bought frozen from Chinese supermarkets. Leave to thaw before steaming.

Energy 241Kcal/1018kJ; Protein 19.1g; Carbohydrate 29.6g, of which sugars 7.5g; Fat 6.3g, of which saturates 1.1g; Cholesterol 83mg; Calcium 92mg; Fibre 2.6g; Sodium 462mg.

MEAT
DISHES

*Meat dishes in Japan and East Asia are normally accompanied
by plenty of vegetables and a staple carbohydrate such as noodles
or rice, providing a balanced and reasonably low-fat meal.
Simmered Beef Slices with Vegetables, and Mongolian Firepot
— an unusual dish that combines lamb with noodles, tofu
and vegetables — illustrate this point perfectly. To keep
the fat content low, it is important that you choose
lean cuts and remove any visible fat.*

SUKIYAKI-STYLE BEEF ★★

THIS JAPANESE DISH IS A MEAL IN ITSELF; THE RECIPE INCORPORATES ALL THE TRADITIONAL ELEMENTS — MEAT, VEGETABLES, NOODLES AND TOFU — IN A HIGHLY FLAVOURED MUSHROOM BROTH.

3 To make the stock, mix together the sugar, rice wine, soy sauce and water in a small bowl.

4 Heat the wok, then add the oil. When the oil is hot, stir-fry the beef for 2–3 minutes until it is cooked, but still pink in colour.

SERVES 4

INGREDIENTS
    450g/1lb lean rump (round) steak
    200g/7oz rice noodles
    15ml/1 tbsp vegetable oil
    200g/7oz firm tofu, cubed
    8 fresh shiitake mushrooms, wiped
      and trimmed
    2 medium leeks, sliced into
      2.5cm/1in lengths
    90g/3½oz baby spinach,
      to serve
For the stock
    15ml/1 tbsp caster (superfine) sugar
    90ml/6 tbsp rice wine
    45ml/3 tbsp dark soy sauce
    120ml/4fl oz/½ cup water

1 Trim off the fat from the beef. If you have time, place it in the freezer and leave for 30 minutes. Cut it into very thin slices.

2 Blanch the noodles in boiling water for 2 minutes. Drain well.

5 Pour the stock over the beef. Add the tofu, mushrooms and leeks. Toss together over the heat for 4 minutes, until the leeks are tender. Meanwhile, wash and thoroughly drain the baby spinach leaves.

6 Serve immediately with the baby spinach leaves, making sure that each person receives some beef and tofu.

Energy 418Kcal/1748kJ; Protein 32.4g; Carbohydrate 42.2g, of which sugars 1.1g; Fat 9.8g, of which saturates 2.5g; Cholesterol 66mg; Calcium 307mg; Fibre 0.7g; Sodium 377mg.

BEEF WITH TOMATOES ★★

BASED ON A SIMPLE KOREAN DISH, THIS COLOURFUL AND FRESH-TASTING MIXTURE IS THE PERFECT WAY OF SERVING SUN-RIPENED TOMATOES FROM THE GARDEN OR FARMERS' MARKET.

SERVES 4

INGREDIENTS

350g/12oz lean rump (round) steak, trimmed of fat
15ml/1 tbsp vegetable oil
300ml/½ pint/1¼ cups beef stock
1 garlic clove, finely chopped
1 small onion, sliced into rings
5 tomatoes, quartered
15ml/1 tbsp tomato purée (paste)
5ml/1 tsp caster (superfine) sugar
15ml/1 tbsp dry sherry
15ml/1 tbsp cold water
salt and ground white pepper
noodles, to serve

1 Slice the rump steak thinly. Place the steak slices in a bowl, add 5ml/1 tsp of the vegetable oil and stir to coat.

2 Bring the stock to the boil in a large pan. Add the beef and cook for 2 minutes, stirring constantly. Drain the beef and set it aside.

VARIATION
Add 5–10ml/1–2 tsp soy sauce to the tomato purée (paste). You will not need to add any extra salt.

3 Heat the remaining oil in a non-stick frying pan or wok until very hot. Stir-fry the garlic and onion for a few seconds.

COOK'S TIP
Use plum tomatoes or vine tomatoes from the garden, if you can. The store-bought ones are a little more expensive than standard tomatoes but have a far better flavour.

4 Add the beef to the pan or wok, then tip in the tomatoes. Stir-fry for 1 minute more over high heat.

5 Mix the tomato purée, sugar, sherry and water in a cup or small bowl. Stir into the pan or wok, add salt and pepper to taste and mix thoroughly. Cook for 1 minute until the sauce is hot. Serve in heated bowls, with noodles.

Energy 172Kcal/723kJ; Protein 20.5g; Carbohydrate 6.7g, of which sugars 6.4g; Fat 6.8g, of which saturates 1.9g; Cholesterol 52mg; Calcium 18mg; Fibre 1.6g; Sodium 74mg.

SIMMERED BEEF SLICES AND VEGETABLES ★★

THIS ONE-POT DISH IS A FAMILY FAVOURITE IN JAPAN. IT IS A GOOD EXAMPLE OF HOW A SMALL
AMOUNT OF MEAT CAN BE STRETCHED WITH VEGETABLES TO MAKE A TASTY LOW-FAT MEAL.

SERVES 4

INGREDIENTS
    250g/9oz lean fillet (beef tenderloin)
      or rump (round) steak, trimmed of
      fat and very thinly sliced
    1 large onion
    15ml/1 tbsp vegetable oil
    450g/1lb small potatoes, halved
      then soaked in water
    1 carrot, cut into 5mm/¼in rounds
    45ml/3 tbsp frozen peas, thawed
      and blanched for 1 minute
For the seasonings
    30ml/2 tbsp caster (superfine) sugar
    75ml/5 tbsp shoyu
    15ml/1 tbsp mirin
    15ml/1 tbsp sake or dry sherry

1 Cut the thinly sliced beef slices into
2cm/¾in wide strips, and slice the
onion lengthways into 5mm/¼in pieces.

2 Heat the vegetable oil in a pan and
lightly fry the beef and onion slices.
When the colour of the meat changes,
drain the potatoes and add to the pan.

3 Once the potatoes are coated with the
oil in the pan, add the carrot. Pour in
just enough water to cover, then bring
to the boil, skimming a few times.

4 Boil vigorously for 2 minutes, then
rearrange the ingredients so that the
potatoes are underneath the beef
and vegetables. Reduce the heat to
medium-low and add all the seasonings.
Simmer for 20 minutes, partially
covered, or until most of the liquid
has evaporated.

5 Check if the potatoes are cooked. Add
the peas and cook to heat through, then
remove the pan from the heat. Serve
the beef and vegetables immediately
in four small serving bowls.

Energy 263Kcal/1110kJ; Protein 17.8g; Carbohydrate 34.7g, of which sugars 15.6g; Fat 6g, of which saturates 1.6g; Cholesterol 37mg; Calcium 37mg; Fibre 2.8g; Sodium 1393mg.

PAPER-THIN SLICED BEEF IN STOCK ★★★

THIS DISH IS GREAT FOR SHARING WITH FRIENDS, AS THE COOKING IS DONE AT THE TABLE. THE SESAME SAUCE THAT USUALLY ACCOMPANIES IT HAS BEEN OMITTED HERE BECAUSE IT IS HIGH IN FAT.

SERVES 4

INGREDIENTS

600g/1⅓lb lean rump (round) steak
2 thin leeks, trimmed and cut into
  thin strips
4 spring onions (scallions), quartered
8 shiitake mushrooms, minus stems
175g/6oz/2 cups oyster mushrooms,
  base part removed, torn into
  small pieces
½ head Chinese leaves (Chinese
  cabbage), cut into 5cm/2in squares
300g/11oz *shungiku*, halved
275g/10oz firm tofu, halved
  and cut crossways in 2cm/¾in
  thick slices
10 x 6cm/4 x 2½in *dashi-konbu*,
  wiped with a damp cloth
For the lime sauce
1 lime
20ml/4 tsp mirin
60ml/4 tbsp rice vinegar
120ml/4fl oz/½ cup shoyu
4 x 6cm/1½ x 2½in *dashi-konbu*
5g/1/8oz *kezuri-bushi*
For the pink daikon
1 piece daikon (mooli), 6cm/2½in
  in length, peeled
1 dried chilli, seeded and cut
  in strips

1 Make the lime sauce. Squeeze the lime into a liquid measure and make up to 120ml/4fl oz/½ cup with water.

2 Pour the lime juice into a small bowl and add the mirin, rice vinegar, shoyu, *dashi-konbu* and *kezuri-bushi*. Cover with clear film (plastic wrap) and leave to stand overnight.

3 Make the pink daikon. Using a wooden skewer, pierce the daikon in several places and insert the chilli strips. Leave for 20 minutes, then grate finely into a sieve (strainer). Squeeze out the liquid and divide among four small bowls.

4 Slice the meat very thinly and arrange on a platter. Put the vegetables and tofu on another platter. Fill a flameproof casserole three-quarters full of water and add the dashi-konbu. Bring to the boil, then transfer to a table burner. Strain the citrus sauce and add 45ml/ 3 tbsp to each bowl of grated daikon.

5 Remove the konbu from the stock. Add some tofu and vegetables to the pot. Each guest picks up a slice of beef, holds it in the stock for a few seconds until cooked, then dips it in the sauce. As the tofu and vegetables are cooked, they are removed and dipped in the same way, and more are added to the pot.

Energy 311Kcal/1302kJ; Protein 40.7g; Carbohydrate 7.1g, of which sugars 6g; Fat 12.9g, of which saturates 4.7g; Cholesterol 92mg; Calcium 412mg; Fibre 3.8g; Sodium 887mg.

ROASTED AND MARINATED PORK ★★

JAPANESE COOKS OFTEN USE A SOY SAUCE AND CITRUS MARINADE TO FLAVOUR MEAT, ADDING IT BEFORE OR AFTER COOKING. IF POSSIBLE, LEAVE THE MEAT TO MARINATE OVERNIGHT.

SERVES 4

INGREDIENTS
600g/1⅓lb pork fillet (tenderloin)
1 garlic clove, crushed
generous pinch of salt
4 spring onions (scallions), trimmed, white part only
10g/¼oz dried wakame seaweed, soaked in water for 20 minutes and drained
10cm/4in celery stick, trimmed and cut in half crossways
1 carton mustard and cress (fine curled cress)
For the sauce
105ml/7 tbsp shoyu
45ml/3 tbsp sake
60ml/4 tbsp mirin
1 lime, sliced into thin rings

1 Preheat the oven to 200°C/400°F/ Gas 6. Rub the pork with crushed garlic and salt, and leave for 15 minutes.

2 Roast the pork for 20 minutes, then turn the meat over and reduce the oven temperature to 180°C/350°F/ Gas 4. Cook for a further 20 minutes, or until the pork is cooked and there are no pink juices when it is pierced.

3 Meanwhile, mix the sauce ingredients in a container that is big enough to hold the pork.

4 When the meat is completely cooked, immediately put it in the sauce, and leave it to marinate for at least 2 hours, or overnight.

5 Cut the white part of the spring onions in half crossways, then in half lengthways. Remove the round cores, then lay the spring onion quarters flat on a chopping board. Slice them very thinly lengthways to make fine shreds.

6 Soak the shreds of spring onion in a bowl of ice-cold water. Repeat with the remaining parts of the spring onions. When the shreds curl up, drain and gather them into a loose ball.

7 Cut the drained wakame seaweed into 2.5cm/1in squares or narrow strips.

8 Slice the trimmed celery very thinly lengthways. Soak in cold water. When the shreds curl up, drain and gather them into a loose ball.

9 Remove the pork from the marinade and wipe it with kitchen paper to soak up any excess. Slice the pork into slices of medium thickness.

10 Strain the marinade into a gravy boat or jug (pitcher).

11 Arrange the sliced pork on a large serving plate and place the vegetables around it. Serve cold with the sauce.

Energy 198Kcal/830kJ; Protein 32.6g; Carbohydrate 0.9g, of which sugars 0.9g; Fat 6.2g, of which saturates 2.1g; Cholesterol 95mg; Calcium 24mg; Fibre 0.4g; Sodium 114mg.

CHAR-SIU PORK ★

LEAN PORK FILLET OR TENDERLOIN IS A DENSE MEAT, SO A LITTLE GOES A LONG WAY. IT TASTES
WONDERFUL WHEN MARINATED, ROASTED AND GLAZED WITH HONEY, AND CAN BE SERVED HOT OR COLD.

SERVES 6

INGREDIENTS

15ml/1 tbsp vegetable oil
15ml/1 tbsp hoisin sauce
15ml/1 tbsp yellow bean sauce
1.5ml/¼ tsp five-spice powder
2.5ml/½ tsp cornflour (cornstarch)
15ml/1 tbsp caster
  (superfine) sugar
1.5ml/¼ tsp salt
1.5ml/¼ tsp ground white pepper
450g/1lb pork fillet (tenderloin),
  trimmed of fat
10ml/2 tsp clear honey
shredded spring onion (scallion),
  to garnish
rice, to serve

1 Mix the oil, sauces, five-spice powder, cornflour, sugar and seasoning in a shallow dish. Add the pork and coat it with the mixture. Cover and chill for 4 hours or overnight.

2 Preheat the oven to 190°C/375°F/ Gas 5. Drain the pork and place it on a wire rack over a deep roasting pan. Roast for 40 minutes, turning the pork over from time to time.

3 Check that the pork is cooked by inserting a skewer or fork into the meat; the juices should run clear. If they are still tinged with pink, roast the pork for 5–10 minutes more.

4 Remove the pork from the oven and brush it with the honey. Leave to cool for 10 minutes before cutting into thin slices. Garnish with spring onion and serve hot or cold with rice.

Energy 117Kcal/491kJ; Protein 16.1g; Carbohydrate 2.4g, of which sugars 2g; Fat 4.8g, of which saturates 1.3g; Cholesterol 47mg; Calcium 6mg; Fibre 0g; Sodium 94mg.

MONGOLIAN FIREPOT ★★

IT IS WORTH INVESTING IN AN AUTHENTIC HOTPOT OR FIREPOT, JUST TO SEE THE DELIGHT ON YOUR GUESTS' FACES WHEN THEY SPY WHAT YOU HAVE IN STORE FOR THEM. THIS TASTES GREAT TOO.

SERVES 6–8

INGREDIENTS
    750g/1⅔lb boned leg of lamb,
      preferably bought thinly sliced
    225g/8oz lamb's liver and/or kidneys
    900ml/1½ pints/3¾ cups lamb stock
      (see Cook's Tip)
    900ml/1½ pints/3¾ cups
      chicken stock
    1cm/½in piece fresh root ginger,
      peeled and thinly sliced
    45ml/3 tbsp rice wine or
      medium-dry sherry
    ½ head Chinese leaves
      (Chinese cabbage), rinsed
      and shredded
    100g/3½oz young spinach leaves
    250g/9oz fresh firm tofu, diced
    115g/4oz cellophane noodles
    salt and ground black pepper
For the dipping sauce
    50ml/2fl oz/¼ cup red
      wine vinegar
    7.5ml/½ tbsp dark soy sauce
    1cm/½in piece fresh root ginger,
      peeled and finely shredded
    1 spring onion (scallion),
      finely shredded
To serve
    bowls of tomato sauce, sweet
      chilli sauce, mustard oil
      and sesame oil
    dry-fried coriander seeds, crushed

COOK'S TIP
When buying the lamb, ask the butcher for the bones and make your own lamb stock. Rinse the bones and place them in a large pan with water to cover. Bring to the boil and skim the surface well. Add 1 peeled onion, 2 peeled carrots, 1cm/½in piece of peeled and bruised ginger, 5ml/1 tsp salt and ground black pepper to taste. Bring back to the boil, then simmer for about an hour until the stock is full of flavour. Strain, leave to cool, then skim and use.

1 Ask the butcher from whom you buy the lamb to slice it thinly on a slicing machine. If you have had to buy the lamb in one piece, however, trim off any fat, then put the leg in the freezer for about an hour, so that it is easier to slice thinly.

2 Trim the liver and remove the skin and core from the kidneys, if using. Place them in the freezer too. If you managed to buy sliced lamb, keep it in the refrigerator until needed.

3 Mix both types of stock in a large pan. Add the sliced ginger and rice wine or sherry, with salt and pepper to taste. Heat to simmering point; simmer for 15 minutes.

4 Slice all the meats thinly and arrange them on a large platter.

5 Place the shredded Chinese leaves, spinach leaves and the diced tofu on a separate platter.

6 Soak the noodles in a bowl of warm or hot water, following the instructions on the packet.

7 Make the dipping sauce by mixing all the ingredients together in a small bowl. The other sauces and the crushed coriander seeds should be spooned into separate small dishes and placed on a serving tray.

8 Fill the moat of the hotpot with the simmering stock. Alternatively, fill a fondue pot and place it over a burner.

9 Each guest selects a portion of meat from the platter and cooks it in the hot stock, using chopsticks or a fondue fork. The meat is then dipped in one of the sauces and coated with the coriander seeds (if you like) before being eaten.

10 When most of the meat has been eaten, top up the stock if necessary, then add the vegetables, tofu and drained noodles.

11 Cook for a minute or two, until the noodles are tender and the vegetables retain a little crispness.

12 Serve the soup in warmed bowls.

Energy 144Kcal/606kJ; Protein 12.3g; Carbohydrate 12g, of which sugars 1.2g; Fat 5.1g, of which saturates 1.1g; Cholesterol 128mg; Calcium 193mg; Fibre 0.9g; Sodium 49mg.

RICE AND NOODLES

This chapter introduces a range of recipes that should be in the repertoire of every low-fat cook. They are universally low in saturated fat, with several dishes registering below 1 gram. Stars in this regard include Five Ingredients Rice and Chilled Somen Noodles. Chicken and Egg on Rice and Lunch-box Rice with Three Toppings are designed to stand alone, while others, such as Red Rice Wrapped in Oak Leaves or Sesame Noodle Salad can be served as appetizers or accompaniments.

RED RICE WRAPPED IN OAK LEAVES ★★

THIS IS A SAVOURY VERSION OF A POPULAR JAPANESE SWEETMEAT. OAK TREES DON'T SHED THEIR OLD LEAVES UNTIL NEW ONES APPEAR, SO THEY REPRESENT THE CONTINUITY OF FAMILY LIFE.

SERVES 4

INGREDIENTS
    65g/2½oz/⅓ cup dried aduki beans
    5ml/1 tsp salt
    300g/11oz/1½ cups glutinous rice
    50g/2oz/¼ cup Japanese short
      grain rice
    12 *kashiwa* leaves (optional)
For the *goma-shio*
    45ml/3 tbsp sesame seeds (black
      sesame, if available)
    5ml/1 tsp ground sea salt

1 Put the aduki beans in a heavy pan and pour in 400ml/14fl oz/1⅔ cups plus 20ml/4 tsp water.

2 Bring to the boil, reduce the heat and simmer, covered, for 20–30 minutes, or until the beans look swollen but are still firm. Remove from the heat and drain. Reserve the liquid in a bowl and add the salt. Return the beans to the pan.

3 Wash all of the rice. Drain in a sieve (strainer) and leave for 30 minutes.

4 Bring another 400ml/14fl oz/1⅔ cups plus 20ml/4 tsp water to the boil. Add to the beans and boil, then simmer for 30 minutes. The beans' skins should start to crack. Drain and add the liquid to the bowl with the reserved liquid. Cover the beans and leave to cool.

5 Add the rice to the bean liquid. Leave to soak for 4–5 hours. Drain the rice and reserve the liquid. Mix the rice into the beans.

6 Bring a steamer of water to the boil. Turn off the heat. Place a tall glass in the centre of the steaming compartment. Pour the rice and beans into the steamer and gently pull the glass out. The hole in the middle will allow even distribution of the steam. Steam on high for 10 minutes.

7 Using your fingers, sprinkle the rice mixture with the reserved liquid from the bowl. Cover again and repeat the process twice more at 10 minute intervals, then leave to steam for 15 minutes more. Remove from the heat. Leave to stand for 10 minutes.

8 Make the *goma-shio*. Roast the sesame seeds and salt in a dry frying pan until the seeds start to pop. Leave to cool, then put in a small dish.

9 Wipe each *kashiwa* leaf with a wet dish towel. Scoop 120ml/4fl oz/½ cup of the rice mixture into a wet tea cup and press with wet fingers. Turn the cup upside down and shape the moulded rice with your hands into a flat ball. Insert into a leaf folded in two. Repeat this process until all the leaves are used. Alternatively, transfer the red rice to a large bowl wiped with a wet towel.

10 Serve the red rice with a sprinkle of *goma-shio*. The kashiwa leaves (except for fresh ones) are edible.

Energy 432Kcal/1807kJ; Protein 12.4g; Carbohydrate 78.7g, of which sugars 0.5g; Fat 7.2g, of which saturates 1g; Cholesterol 0mg; Calcium 105mg; Fibre 2.2g; Sodium 5mg.

FIVE INGREDIENTS RICE ★

THE JAPANESE LOVE RICE SO MUCH THEY INVENTED MANY WAYS TO ENJOY IT. HERE, CHICKEN AND VEGETABLES ARE COOKED WITH SHORT GRAIN RICE MAKING A HEALTHY LIGHT LUNCH DISH.

SERVES 4

INGREDIENTS

275g/10oz/1¼ cups Japanese
    short grain rice
90g/3½oz carrot, peeled
2.5ml/½ tsp lemon juice
90g/3½oz gobo (burdock) or canned
    bamboo shoots
225g/8oz/3 cups oyster mushrooms
8 fresh mitsuba or parsley sprigs
350ml/12fl oz/1½ cups water
    and 7.5ml/1½ tsp instant
    dashi powder
150g/5oz skinless chicken breast
    fillet, cut into 2cm/¾in chunks
30ml/2 tbsp shoyu
30ml/2 tbsp sake
25ml/1½ tbsp mirin
pinch of salt

1 Put the rice in a large bowl and wash well with cold water. Keep changing the water until it remains clear, then tip the rice into a sieve (strainer) and drain for 30 minutes.

2 Using a sharp knife, cut the carrot into 5mm/¼in rounds, then cut the discs into flowers.

COOK'S TIP

Although gobo or burdock is recognized as a poisonous plant in the West, it has been eaten in Japan for centuries. To make it safe to eat, gobo must always be cooked, because it contains iron and other acidic elements that are harmful if they are eaten raw. By soaking it in alkaline water and then cooking it for a short time, gobo becomes edible.

3 Fill a small bowl with cold water and add the lemon juice. Peel the gobo and then slice it with a knife as if you were sharpening a pencil into the bowl.

4 Leave for 15 minutes, then drain. If using canned bamboo shoots, slice them into thin matchsticks.

5 Tear the oyster mushrooms into thin strips. Chop the mitsuba or parsley. Put it in a sieve and pour over hot water from the kettle to wilt the leaves. Allow to drain and then set aside.

6 Heat the dashi stock in a large pan and add the carrots and gobo or bamboo shoots. Bring to the boil and add the chicken. Remove any scum from the surface, and add the shoyu, sake, mirin and salt.

7 Add the rice and mushrooms and cover with a tight-fitting lid. Bring back to the boil, wait 5 minutes, then reduce the heat and simmer for 10 minutes. Remove from the heat without lifting the lid and leave to stand for 15 minutes. Add the wilted herbs and serve.

Energy 312Kcal/1308kJ; Protein 16.1g; Carbohydrate 58.4g, of which sugars 2.8g; Fat 1.2g, of which saturates 0.2g; Cholesterol 26mg; Calcium 30mg; Fibre 1.5g; Sodium 566mg.

CHICKEN AND EGG ON RICE ★★

THE AGE-OLD QUESTION OF WHICH CAME FIRST, THE CHICKEN OR THE EGG, IS ADDRESSED IN THIS JAPANESE DISH. IT IS TRADITIONALLY COOKED IN A LIDDED CERAMIC BOWL CALLED A DONI-BURI.

SERVES 4

INGREDIENTS
  250g/9oz skinless, boneless
    chicken thighs
  4 fresh mitsuba or parsley
    sprigs, trimmed
  300ml/½ pint/1¼ cups water
    and 25ml/1½ tbsp instant
    dashi powder
  30ml/2 tbsp caster (superfine) sugar
  60ml/4 tbsp mirin
  60ml/4 tbsp shoyu
  2 small onions, sliced
    thinly lengthways
  4 large (US extra large) eggs, beaten
  275g/10oz/scant 1½ cups Japanese
    short grain rice cooked with 375ml/
    13fl oz/scant 1⅔ cups water
  shichimi togarashi, to serve (optional)

1 Cut the chicken thighs into 2cm/¾in square bitesize chunks. Chop the roots of the fresh mitsuba or parsley into 2.5cm/1in lengths. Set aside.

2 Pour the dashi stock, sugar, mirin and shoyu into a clean frying pan with a lid and bring to the boil. Add the onion slices to the pan and lay the chicken pieces on top. Cook over a high heat for 5 minutes, shaking the pan frequently.

3 When the chicken is cooked, sprinkle with the mitsuba or parsley, and pour the beaten eggs over to cover the chicken. Cover and wait for 30 seconds. Do not stir.

4 Remove from the heat and leave to stand for 1 minute. The egg should be just cooked but still soft, rather than set. Do not leave it so that the egg becomes a firm omelette.

5 Scoop the warm rice on to individual plates, then pour the soft eggs and chicken on to the rice. Serve immediately with a little *shichimi-togarashi*, if you want spicy taste.

COOK'S TIP
Mitsuba, also known as Japanese wild parsley, tastes like angelica. Cut off the root before use.

Energy 417Kcal/1743kJ; Protein 25.2g; Carbohydrate 56.9g, of which sugars 1.9g; Fat 7.8g, of which saturates 2.1g; Cholesterol 256mg; Calcium 70mg; Fibre 0.2g; Sodium 935mg.

LUNCH-BOX RICE <u>WITH</u> THREE TOPPINGS ★★★

A GREAT DEAL MORE NUTRITIOUS THAN SOME OF THE PACKED LUNCHES TAKEN TO SCHOOL IN THE WEST, THIS JAPANESE SPECIALITY TOPS RICE WITH THREE DIFFERENT TOPPINGS.

MAKES 4 LUNCH BOXES

INGREDIENTS
  275g/10oz/scant 1⅔ cups Japanese
    short grain rice cooked using 375ml/
    13fl oz/scant 1⅔ cups water, cooled
  45ml/3 tbsp sesame seeds, toasted
  salt
  3 mangetouts (snow peas), to garnish
For the *iri-tamago* (yellow topping)
  30ml/2 tbsp caster (superfine) sugar
  5ml/1 tsp salt
  3 eggs, beaten
For the *denbu* (pink topping)
  115g/4oz cod fillet, skinned
    and boned
  20ml/4 tsp caster (superfine) sugar
  5ml/1 tsp salt
  5ml/1 tsp sake
  2 drops of red vegetable colouring,
    diluted with a few drops of water
For the *tori-soboro* (beige topping)
  200g/7oz/scant 1 cup minced
    (ground) chicken
  45ml/3 tbsp sake
  15ml/1 tbsp caster (superfine) sugar
  15ml/1 tbsp shoyu
  15ml/1 tbsp water

1 To make the *iri-tamago*, mix the sugar and salt with the eggs in a pan. Cook over a medium heat, stirring with a whisk or fork as you would to scramble eggs. When the mixture is almost set, remove from the heat and stir until the egg becomes fine and slightly dry.

2 To make the *denbu*, cook the cod fillet for 2 minutes in a large pan of boiling water. Drain and dry well with kitchen paper. Skin and remove all the fish bones.

3 Put the cod and sugar into a pan, add the salt and sake, and cook over low heat for 1 minute, stirring with a fork to flake the cod. Reduce the heat to low and sprinkle on the colouring. Continue to stir for 15–20 minutes, or until the cod flakes become very fluffy and fibrous. Transfer the *denbu* to a plate.

4 To make the *tori-soboro*, put the minced chicken, sake, sugar, shoyu and water into a small pan. Cook over medium heat for about 3 minutes, then reduce the heat to medium-low and stir with a fork or whisk until the liquid has almost evaporated.

5 Blanch the mangetouts for about 3 minutes in lightly salted boiling water, drain and carefully slice into fine 3mm/⅛in sticks.

6 Mix the rice with the sesame seeds in a bowl. With a wet spoon, divide the rice among four 17 × 12cm/6½ × 4½in lunch boxes. Flatten the surface using the back of a wooden spoon.

7 Spoon a quarter of the egg into each box to cover a third of the rice. Cover the next third with a quarter of the *denbu*, and the last section with a quarter of the chicken topping. Use the lid to divide the boxes, if you like. Garnish with the mangetout sticks.

Energy 516Kcal/2162kJ; Protein 29.3g; Carbohydrate 72.2g, of which sugars 17.2g; Fat 11.8g, of which saturates 2.3g; Cholesterol 191mg; Calcium 124mg; Fibre 0.9g; Sodium 370mg.

SESAME NOODLE SALAD ★★★

TOASTED SESAME OIL ADDS A NUTTY FLAVOUR TO THIS ASIAN-STYLE SALAD. IT TASTES BEST WHEN IT IS SERVED WARM, AND IT IS SUBSTANTIAL ENOUGH TO SERVE AS A MAIN MEAL.

3 Meanwhile, make the dressing. Whisk together the soy sauce, sesame and sunflower oils, grated ginger and crushed garlic in a small bowl.

4 Cut the tomatoes in half and scoop out the seeds with a teaspoon, then chop roughly. Cut the spring onions into fine shreds.

SERVES 4

INGREDIENTS

    250g/9oz medium egg noodles
    200g/7oz/1¾ cup sugar snap peas
      or mangetouts (snow peas)
    2 tomatoes
    3 spring onions (scallions)
    2 carrots, cut into julienne
    30ml/2 tbsp chopped fresh coriander
      (cilantro)
    15ml/1 tbsp sesame seeds
    fresh coriander (cilantro), to garnish
For the dressing
    10ml/2 tsp light soy sauce
    15ml/1 tbsp toasted sesame seed oil
    15ml/1 tbsp vegetable oil
    4cm/1½in piece fresh root ginger,
      finely grated
    1 garlic clove, crushed

1 Bring a large pan of lightly salted water to the boil. Add the egg noodles, and bring back to the boil. Cook for 2 minutes.

2 Slice the sugar snap peas or mangetouts diagonally, add to the pan and cook for a further 2 minutes. Drain and rinse under cold running water.

5 Tip the noodles and the peas or mangetouts into a large bowl and add the carrots, tomatoes and coriander.

6 Pour the dressing over the top of the noodle mixture, and toss with your hands to combine. Sprinkle with the sesame seeds and top with the spring onions and coriander.

Energy 323Kcal/1364kJ; Protein 10.6g; Carbohydrate 50.1g, of which sugars 5.9g; Fat 10.3g, of which saturates 2.2g; Cholesterol 19mg; Calcium 76mg; Fibre 4.2g; Sodium 301mg.

CHILLED SOMEN NOODLES ★★

AT THE HEIGHT OF SUMMER, COLD SOMEN NOODLES SERVED IN ICE COLD WATER AND ACCOMPANIED BY A DIPPING SAUCE AND A SELECTION OF RELISHES MAKE A REFRESHING MEAL.

SERVES 4

INGREDIENTS
 300g/11oz dried somen noodles
For the dipping sauce
 105ml/7 tbsp mirin
 2.5ml/½ tsp sea salt
 105ml/7 tbsp shoyu
 400ml/14fl oz/1⅔ cups konbu and
  bonito stock or instant dashi
For the relishes
 2 spring onions (scallions), trimmed
  and finely chopped
 2.5cm/1in fresh root ginger, peeled
  and finely grated
 2 fresh shiso or basil leaves, finely
  chopped (optional)
 30ml/2 tbsp toasted sesame seeds
For the garnishes
 10cm/4in cucumber
 5ml/1 tsp sea salt
 ice cubes or a block of ice
 ice-cold water
 115g/4oz cooked, peeled small
  prawns (shrimp)
 orchid flowers or nasturtium flowers
  and leaves (optional)

1 To make the dipping sauce, put the mirin in a pan and bring to the boil to evaporate the alcohol. Add the salt and shoyu and shake the pan gently to mix. Add the kombu and bonito stock or instant dashi. Add the water and bring to the boil. Cook over a vigorous heat for 3 minutes without stirring. Remove from the heat and strain through muslin or cheesecloth. Cool, then chill for at least 1 hour.

2 Prepare the cucumber garnish. If the cucumber is bigger than 4cm/1½in in diameter, cut in half and scoop out the seeds, then slice thinly. For a smaller cucumber, cut into 5cm/2in lengths, then use a vegetable peeler to remove the seeds and make a hole in the centre. Slice thinly.

3 Sprinkle with the salt and leave in a sieve (strainer) for 20 minutes, then rinse in cold water and drain.

4 Bring at least 1.5 litres/2½ pints/ 6 cups water to the boil in a large pan. Have 75ml/2½fl oz/⅓ cup cold water to hand. Put the somen in the rapidly boiling water. When the water foams, pour the glass of cold water in. When the water boils again, the somen are ready. Drain into a colander.

5 Rinse under cold running water, and rub the somen with your hands to remove the starch. Drain well.

6 Put some ice cubes or a block of ice in the centre of a chilled, large glass bowl, and add the somen. Pour on enough ice-cold water to cover the somen, then arrange cucumber slices, prawns and flowers, if using, on top.

7 Prepare all the relishes separately and place them in small dishes or small sake cups.

8 Divide approximately one-third of the dipping sauce among four small cups. Put the remaining sauce in a jug (pitcher) or gravy boat.

9 Serve the noodles cold with the relishes. The guests are invited to put any combination of relishes into their dipping-sauce cup. The cup is then held over the somen bowl, and a mouthful of somen is picked up, dipped into the sauce and eaten. More dipping sauce is added from the jug and more relishes are spooned into the dipping-sauce cups as required.

VEGETABLES AND SALADS

All of the recipes in this chapter are low in fat, especially

saturated fat, but they are also filling and full of flavour, so

you won't feel any sense of sacrifice. You could combine a

couple of dishes, such as New Potatoes Cooked in Dashi Stock

and Slow-cooked Shiitake with Shoyu, and still stay well

within sensible fat limits. If you are looking for a one-dish

meal, try Steamed Aubergine with Sesame Sauce,

or serve Bamboo Shoot Salad as a light meal.

BROCCOLI WITH SOY SAUCE ★

A WONDERFULLY SIMPLE DISH THAT YOU WILL WANT TO MAKE AGAIN AND AGAIN. THE BROCCOLI COOKS IN NEXT TO NO TIME, SO DON'T START COOKING UNTIL YOU ARE ALMOST READY TO EAT.

SERVES 4

INGREDIENTS
    450g/1lb broccoli
    15ml/1 tbsp vegetable oil
    2 garlic cloves, sliced
    30 ml/2 tbsp light soy sauce
    salt

COOK'S TIP
Broccoli is a rich source of vitamin C and folic acid and is also believed to have antioxidant properties.

1 Trim the thick stems of the broccoli and cut the head into large florets.

2 Bring a pan of lightly salted water to the boil. Add the broccoli and cook for 3–4 minutes until crisp-tender.

3 Drain the broccoli thoroughly and transfer it to a heated serving dish.

4 Heat the oil in a small pan. Fry the sliced garlic for 2 minutes to release the flavour, then remove it with a slotted spoon. Pour the oil carefully over the broccoli, taking care as it will splatter.

5 Drizzle the soy sauce over the broccoli, sprinkle over the fried garlic and serve.

VARIATIONS
Cos lettuce or Chinese leaves (Chinese cabbage) taste delicious prepared this way.

Energy 65Kcal/271kJ; Protein 5.2g; Carbohydrate 2.7g, of which sugars 2.2g; Fat 3.8g, of which saturates 0.6g; Cholesterol 0mg; Calcium 64mg; Fibre 2.9g; Sodium 543mg.

STEAMED AUBERGINE <u>WITH</u> SESAME SAUCE ★

SERVE THIS TASTY VEGETABLE MEDLEY ON ITS OWN, OR AS AN ACCOMPANIMENT TO GRILLED STEAK.
IT CONTAINS VERY LITTLE FAT, SO CAN EASILY BE ACCOMMODATED IN A HEALTHY DIET.

SERVES 4

INGREDIENTS
    2 large aubergines (eggplants)
    400ml/14fl oz/1²⁄₃ cups water
      with 5ml/1 tsp instant
      dashi powder
    25ml/1½ tbsp caster
      (superfine) sugar
    15ml/1 tbsp shoyu
    15ml/1 tbsp sesame seeds, finely
      ground in a mortar and pestle
    15ml/1 tbsp sake or dry sherry
    15ml/1 tbsp cornflour (cornstarch)
    salt
For the accompanying vegetables
    130g/4½oz shimeji mushrooms
    115g/4oz/¾ cup fine green beans
    100ml/3fl oz/scant ½ cup water
      with 5ml/1 tsp instant
      dashi powder
    25ml/1½ tbsp caster
      (superfine) sugar
    15ml/1 tbsp sake or dry sherry
    1.5ml/¼ tsp salt
    dash of shoyu

1 Peel the aubergines and cut them in quarters lengthways. Prick them all over with a skewer, then plunge them into a bowl of salted water. Leave them to stand for 30 minutes.

2 Drain the aubergines and lay them side by side in a steamer, or in a wok half filled with simmering water and with a bamboo basket supported on a tripod inside, for 20 minutes, or until the aubergines are soft. If the quarters are too long to fit in the steamer, cut them in half.

3 Mix the dashi stock, sugar, shoyu and 1.5ml/¼ tsp salt together in a large pan. Gently transfer the aubergines to this pan, then cover and cook over a low heat for a further 15 minutes. Take a few tablespoonfuls of stock from the pan and mix with the ground sesame seeds. Add this mixture to the pan.

4 Thoroughly mix the sake with the cornflour in small bowl, then add to the pan with the aubergines and stock and shake the pan gently, but quickly. When the sauce becomes quite thick, remove the pan from the heat.

5 While the aubergines are cooking, prepare and cook the accompanying vegetables. Wash the mushrooms and cut off the hard base part. Separate the large block into smaller chunks with your fingers. Trim the green beans and cut in half.

6 Mix the stock with the sugar, sake, salt and shoyu in a shallow pan. Add the green beans and mushrooms and cook for 7 minutes until just tender. Serve the aubergines and their sauce in individual bowls with the accompanying vegetables over the top.

Energy 93Kcal/390kJ; Protein 2.9g; Carbohydrate 13.6g, of which sugars 9.6g; Fat 2.9g, of which saturates 0.5g; Cholesterol 0mg; Calcium 52mg; Fibre 3.3g; Sodium 274mg.

SLOW-COOKED SHIITAKE WITH SHOYU ★★

SHIITAKE MUSHROOMS COOKED SLOWLY ARE SO RICH AND FILLING, THAT SOME PEOPLE CALL THEM "VEGETARIAN STEAK". THIS IS A USEFUL AND FLAVOURSOME ADDITION TO OTHER DISHES.

SERVES 4

INGREDIENTS
    20 dried shiitake mushrooms
    30ml/2 tbsp vegetable oil
    30ml/2 tbsp shoyu
    5ml/1 tsp toasted sesame oil

1 Start soaking the dried shiitake the day before. Put them in a large bowl almost full of water. Cover the shiitake with a plate or lid to stop them floating to the surface of the water. Leave to soak overnight.

VARIATION
Cut the slow-cooked shiitake into thin strips. Mix with 600g/1⅓lb/5¼ cups cooked brown rice and 15ml/1 tbsp finely chopped chives. Sprinkle with toasted sesame seeds.

2 Remove the shiitake from the soaking water and gently squeeze out the water with your fingers.

3 Measure 120ml/4fl oz/½ cup of the liquid in the bowl, and set aside.

4 Heat the oil in a wok or a large frying pan. Stir-fry the shiitake over a high heat for 5 minutes, stirring continuously.

5 Reduce the heat to the lowest setting, then add the liquid and the shoyu.

6 Cook the mushrooms until there is almost no moisture left, stirring frequently. Sprinkle with the toasted sesame oil and remove from the heat.

7 Leave to cool, then slice and arrange the shiitake on a large plate.

Energy 66Kcal/272kJ; Protein 1.1g; Carbohydrate 0.8g, of which sugars 0.7g; Fat 6.5g, of which saturates 0.8g; Cholesterol 0mg; Calcium 4mg; Fibre 0.6g; Sodium 537mg.

NEW POTATOES COOKED IN DASHI STOCK ★

As the stock evaporates in this delicious dish, the onion becomes meltingly soft and caramelized, making a wonderful sauce that coats the potatoes.

SERVES 4

INGREDIENTS

15ml/1 tbsp toasted sesame oil
1 small onion, thinly sliced
1kg/2¼lb baby new
   potatoes, unpeeled
200ml/7fl oz/scant 1 cup water with
   5ml/1 tsp instant dashi powder
45ml/3 tbsp shoyu

COOK'S TIP
Japanese chefs use toasted sesame oil for its distinctive strong aroma. If the smell is too strong, use a mixture of half sesame and half vegetable oil.

1 Heat the sesame oil in a wok or large pan. Add the onion slices and stir-fry for 30 seconds, then add the potatoes. Stir constantly, until all the potatoes are well coated in sesame oil, and have begun to sizzle.

2 Pour on the dashi stock and shoyu and reduce the heat to the lowest setting. Cover and cook for 15 minutes, turning the potatoes every 5 minutes so that they cook evenly.

3 Uncover the wok or pan for a further 5 minutes to reduce the liquid. If there is already very little liquid remaining, remove the wok or pan from the heat, cover and leave to stand for 5 minutes. Check that the potatoes are cooked, then remove from the heat.

4 Transfer the potatoes and onions to a deep serving bowl. Pour the sauce over the top and serve immediately.

Energy 210Kcal/890kJ; Protein 4.8g; Carbohydrate 42.4g, of which sugars 4.9g; Fat 3.5g, of which saturates 0.7g; Cholesterol 0mg; Calcium 21mg; Fibre 2.7g; Sodium 829mg.

BAMBOO SHOOT SALAD ★

THIS HOT, SHARP-FLAVOURED SALAD IS POPULAR THROUGHOUT EAST ASIA. USE CANNED WHOLE BAMBOO SHOOTS, IF YOU CAN FIND THEM — THEY HAVE MORE FLAVOUR THAN SLICED ONES.

SERVES 4

INGREDIENTS

    400g/14oz canned bamboo shoots,
      in large pieces
    25g/1oz/about 3 tbsp glutinous rice
    30ml/2 tbsp chopped shallots
    15ml/1 tbsp chopped garlic
    45ml/3 tbsp chopped spring
      onions (scallions)
    30ml/2 tbsp Thai fish sauce
    30ml/2 tbsp fresh lime juice
    5ml/1 tsp sugar
    2.5ml/½ tsp dried chilli flakes
    20–25 small fresh mint leaves
    15ml/1 tbsp toasted sesame seeds

COOK'S TIP
Glutinous rice does not, in fact, contain any gluten – it's just sticky.

1 Rinse the bamboo shoots under cold running water, then drain them and pat them thoroughly dry with kitchen paper and set them aside.

2 Dry-roast the rice in a frying pan until it is golden brown. Leave to cool slightly, then tip into a mortar and grind to fine crumbs with a pestle.

3 Transfer the rice to a bowl and add the shallots, garlic, spring onions, fish sauce, lime juice, sugar, chillies and half the mint leaves. Mix well.

4 Add the bamboo shoots to the bowl and toss to mix. Serve sprinkled with the toasted sesame seeds and the remaining mint leaves.

Energy 88Kcal/368kJ; Protein 4.4g; Carbohydrate 11.5g, of which sugars 4.6g; Fat 2.8g, of which saturates 0.4g; Cholesterol 0mg; Calcium 51mg; Fibre 2g; Sodium 274mg.

JAPANESE SALAD ★★

HIJIKI IS A MILD-TASTING SEAWEED AND, COMBINED WITH RADISHES, CUCUMBER AND BEANSPROUTS, IT MAKES A REFRESHING SALAD THAT IS THE PERFECT ACCOMPANIMENT TO A RICH MAIN DISH.

SERVES 4

INGREDIENTS
 15g/½oz/½ cup hijiki seaweed
 250g/9oz/1¼ cups radishes, sliced
   into very thin rounds
 1 small cucumber, cut into
   thin sticks
 75g/3oz/1½ cups beansprouts
For the dressing
 15ml/1 tbsp sunflower oil
 15ml/1 tbsp toasted sesame oil
 5ml/1 tsp light soy sauce
 30ml/2 tbsp rice vinegar or 15ml/
   1 tbsp wine vinegar
 15ml/1 tbsp mirin

1 Soak the hijiki in a bowl of cold water for 10–15 minutes until it is rehydrated, then drain, rinse under cold running water and drain again. It should almost triple in volume.

2 Place the hijiki in a pan of water. Bring the water to the boil, then reduce the heat and simmer the hijiki for about 30 minutes or until tender.

COOK'S TIP
Hijiki is a type of seaweed that is popular in Japan. It resembles wakame and is generally sold dried and finely shredded. It is available in many supermarkets and Asian stores.

3 Meanwhile, make the dressing. Whisk the oils with the vinegar and mirin in a bowl until combined, and then whisk in the soy sauce.

4 Drain the cooked hijiki in a sieve (strainer) and arrange it in a shallow bowl or platter with the prepared radishes, cucumber and beansprouts. Pour over the dressing and toss lightly to combine.

Energy 68Kcal/280kJ; Protein 1.4g; Carbohydrate 2.8g, of which sugars 2.4g; Fat 5.8g, of which saturates 0.8g; Cholesterol 0mg; Calcium 23mg; Fibre 1.1g; Sodium 276mg.

SWEET
SNACKS

*Desserts have never been central to culinary tradition in
Japan and East Asia. At the conclusion of a meal you are
more likely to be offered fresh fruit than a fancy sweet dish.
The Japanese tend to use rice, vegetables and dried beans,
including kabocha squash and aduki beans, in combination
with exotic fruit, such as mango, kiwi fruit or Asian pears,
to create unusual sweet snacks. Star examples are Exotic
Fruit Sushi or Kabocha Squash Cake.*

KABOCHA SQUASH CAKE ★

THIS IS A VERY SWEET JAPANESE DESSERT OFTEN MADE WITH ADUKI BEANS, TO BE EATEN AT TEA TIME WITH GREEN TEA. THE BITTERNESS OF THE TEA BALANCES THE SWEETNESS OF THE CAKE.

2 Steam the kabocha squash in a covered steamer for about 15 minutes over a medium heat. It will be ready when a chopstick or skewer can be pushed into the centre easily. Remove and leave, covered, for 5 minutes.

3 Remove the skin from the kabocha. Mash the flesh and push it through a sieve (strainer) using a wooden spoon, or purée it in a blender or food processor. Scrape the purée into a mixing bowl. Add the flour, cornflour, caster sugar, cinnamon, water and beaten egg yolks. Mix well.

4 Roll out a *makisu sushi* mat as you would if making a *sushi* roll. Wet some muslin or cheesecloth slightly with water and lay it on the mat. Spread the kabocha cake mixture evenly on the wet cloth. Hold the nearest end and tightly roll up the *makisu* to the other end. Close both outer ends by rolling up or folding the cloth over.

5 Put the *makisu* containing the rolled kabocha cake back into the steamer for 5 minutes. Remove from the heat and leave to set for 5 minutes.

6 If serving with fruit, peel, trim and slice the Asian pear and persimmon very thinly lengthways.

7 Open the *makisu* when the roll has cooled down. Cut the cake into 2.5cm/1in thick slices and serve cold on four small plates with the thinly sliced fruit, if using.

SERVES 4

INGREDIENTS
  1 × 350g/12oz kabocha squash
  30ml/2 tbsp plain
    (all-purpose) flour
  15ml/1 tbsp cornflour (cornstarch)
  10ml/2 tsp caster (superfine) sugar
  1.5ml/¼ tsp salt
  1.5ml/¼ tsp ground cinnamon
  25ml/1½ tbsp water
  2 egg yolks, beaten
To serve (optional)
  ½ Asian pear
  ½ persimmon

1 Cut off the hard part from the top and bottom of the kabocha, then cut it into three to four wedges. Scoop out the seeds with a spoon. Cut into chunks.

Energy 97Kcal/409kJ; Protein 4.5g; Carbohydrate 13.8g, of which sugars 4.2g; Fat 3.1g, of which saturates 0.9g; Cholesterol 95mg; Calcium 52mg; Fibre 1.1g; Sodium 37mg.

EXOTIC FRUIT *SUSHI* ★

THIS IDEA CAN BE ADAPTED TO INCORPORATE A WIDE VARIETY OF FRUITS, BUT TO KEEP TO THE EXOTIC THEME TAKE YOUR INSPIRATION FROM THE TROPICS. THE SUSHI NEEDS TO CHILL OVERNIGHT.

SERVES 4

INGREDIENTS
    150g/5oz/⅔ cup short grain
        pudding rice
    350ml/12fl oz/1½ cups water
    400ml/14fl oz/1⅔ cups reduced-fat
        coconut milk
    75g/3oz/⅓ cup caster
        (superfine) sugar
    a selection of exotic fruit, such as
        1 mango, 1 kiwi fruit, 2 figs and
        1 star fruit (carambola),
        thinly sliced
    30ml/2 tbsp apricot jam, sieved
For the raspberry sauce
    225g/8oz/2 cups raspberries
    25g/1oz/¼ cup icing
        (confectioners') sugar

1 Rinse the rice well under cold running water, drain and place in a pan with 300ml/½ pint/1¼ cups of the water. Pour in 175ml/6fl oz/¾ cup of the coconut milk. Cook over very low heat for 25 minutes, stirring often and gradually adding the remaining coconut milk, until the rice has absorbed all the liquid and is tender.

2 Grease a shallow 18cm/7in square tin (pan) and line it with clear film (plastic wrap). Stir 30ml/2 tbsp of the caster sugar into the rice mixture and pour it into the prepared tin. Cool, then chill overnight.

COOK'S TIP
To cut the rice mixture into bars, turn out of the tin, cut in half lengthways, then make 7 crossways cuts for 16 bars. Shape into ovals with damp hands.

3 Cut the rice mixture into 16 small bars, shape into ovals and flatten the tops. Place on a baking sheet lined with baking parchment. Arrange the sliced fruit on top, using one type of fruit only for each *sushi*.

4 Place the remaining sugar in a small pan with the remaining 60ml/4 tbsp water. Bring to the boil, then lower the heat and simmer until the liquid becomes thick and syrupy. Stir in the jam and cool slightly.

5 To make the raspberry sauce, put the raspberries in a food processor or blender, and add the icing sugar. Process in short bursts, using the pulse button if your machine has one, until the raspberries are a purée. Press through a sieve, then divide among four small bowls.

6 Arrange a few different fruit *sushi* on each plate and spoon over a little of the cool apricot syrup. Serve with the raspberry sauce.

Energy 323Kcal/1372kJ; Protein 4.5g; Carbohydrate 77.1g, of which sugars 47g; Fat 0.8g, of which saturates 0.3g; Cholesterol 0mg; Calcium 73mg; Fibre 2.9g; Sodium 118mg.

SWEET ADUKI BEAN PASTE JELLY ★

BASED ON AGAR-AGAR, A SETTING AGENT MADE FROM SEAWEED, THESE JELLIES LOOK LIKE BLOCKS OF MOUNTAIN ICE IN WHICH SEMI-PRECIOUS STONES HAVE BEEN TRAPPED FOR CENTURIES.

SERVES 12

INGREDIENTS
200g/7oz can aduki beans
40g/1½oz/3 tbsp caster
   (superfine) sugar
For the *agar-agar* jelly
   2 × 5g/⅛oz sachets powdered
      agar-agar
   100g/3¾oz/½ cup caster sugar
   rind of ¼ orange in one piece

1 Drain the beans, then tip into a pan over a medium heat. When steam begins to rise, reduce the heat to low.

2 Add the sugar one-third at a time, stirring constantly until the sugar has dissolved and the moisture evaporated. Remove from the heat.

3 Pour 450ml/¾ pint/scant 2 cups water into a pan, and mix with one *agar-agar* sachet. Stir until dissolved, then add 40g/1½oz of the sugar and the orange rind. Bring to the boil and cook for about 2 minutes, stirring constantly until the sugar has all dissolved.

4 Remove from the heat and discard the orange rind.

5 Transfer 250ml/8fl oz/1 cup of the hot liquid into a 15 × 10cm/6 × 4in container so that it fills only 1cm/½in. Leave at room temperature to set.

6 Add the bean paste to the *agar-agar* liquid in the pan, and mix well. Move the pan on to a wet dish towel and keep stirring for 8 minutes.

7 Pour the bean and *agar-agar* liquid into an 18 × 7.5 × 2cm/7 × 3 × ¾in container and leave to set for 1 hour at room temperature, then 1 hour in the refrigerator. Turn upside down on to a chopping board covered with kitchen paper. Leave for 1 minute, then cut into 12 rectangular pieces.

8 Line 12 ramekins with clear film (plastic wrap). With a fork, cut the set kanten block into 12 squares. Put one square in each ramekin, then place a bean and kanten cube on top of each.

9 Pour 450ml/¾ pint/scant 2 cups water into a pan and mix with the remaining kanten sachet. Bring to the boil, add the remaining sugar, then stir constantly until dissolved. Boil for a further 2 minutes, and remove from the heat. Place the pan on a wet dish towel to cool quickly and stir for 5 minutes, or until the liquid starts to thicken.

10 Ladle the liquid into the ramekins to cover the cubes. Twist the clear film at the top. Leave to set in the refrigerator for at least 1 hour. Carefully remove the ramekins and clear film and serve cold on serving plates.

Energy 63Kcal/267kJ; Protein 1.2g; Carbohydrate 15.2g, of which sugars 12.8g; Fat 0.1g, of which saturates 0g; Cholesterol 0mg; Calcium 18mg; Fibre 1g; Sodium 66mg.

STICKY RICE IN BEAN PASTE ★

THIS TEA-TIME SNACK IS AN ABSOLUTE FAVOURITE AMONG ALL AGES IN JAPAN. IT IS ALSO MADE ON OCCASIONS SUCH AS BIRTHDAYS AND FESTIVALS, WHEN IT IS DECORATED WITH CAMELLIA LEAVES.

MAKES 12

INGREDIENTS

   150g/5oz/scant 1 cup glutinous rice
   50g/2oz/1⁄3 cup Japanese short
    grain rice
   410g/14 1⁄4 oz can aduki beans
    (canned in water, with sugar and salt)
   90g/3 1⁄2 oz/6 1⁄2 tbsp caster
    (superfine) sugar
   pinch of salt

1 Mix both kinds of rice in a sieve (strainer), wash well under running water, then drain. Leave for at least 1 hour to dry.

2 Tip the rice into a heavy cast-iron pan or flameproof casserole with a lid, and add 200ml/7fl oz/scant 1 cup water.

3 Cover and bring to the boil, then reduce the heat to low and simmer for 15 minutes, or until a slight crackling noise is heard from the pan.

4 Remove from the heat and leave to stand for 5 minutes. Remove the lid, cover and leave to cool.

5 Pour the contents of the aduki bean can into a pan and cook over a medium heat. Add the sugar a third at a time, mixing well after each addition.

6 Reduce the heat to low and mash the beans using a potato masher. Add the salt and remove from the heat. The consistency should be like that of mashed potatoes. Heat gently to remove any excess liquid. Leave to cool.

7 Wet your hands. Shape the sticky rice into 12 balls, each about the size of a golf ball.

8 Dampen some muslin or cheesecloth and place on the work surface.

9 Scoop up 30ml/2 tbsp of the aduki bean paste and spread it in the centre of the cloth to a thickness of about 5mm/1⁄4in.

COOK'S TIP
Make sure the muslin or cheesecloth is really damp, or the rice mixture will stick to it and prove difficult to remove.

10 Put a rice ball in the middle, then wrap it up in the paste using the muslin. Open the cloth and remove the ball. Repeat until all the rice balls are used up. Serve at room temperature.

Energy 123Kcal/518kJ; Protein 3.6g; Carbohydrate 27.1g, of which sugars 9g; Fat 0.3g, of which saturates 0g; Cholesterol 0mg; Calcium 31mg; Fibre 2.1g; Sodium 130mg.

INDEX

ACKNOWLEDGEMENTS

Recipes Catherine Atkinson, Alex Barker, Ghillie Basan, Judy Bastyra, Carla Capalbo, Kit Chan, Roz Denny, Joanna Farrow, Rafi Fernandez, Christine France, Silvano Franco, Linda Fraser, Yasuko Fukuoka, Elaine Gardner, Sarah Gates, Shirley Gill, Brian Glover, Nicola Graimes, Deh-Ta Hsiung, Shehzad Husain, Christine Ingram, Becky Johnson, Emi Kazuko, Soheila Kimberley, Lucy Knox, Masaki Ko, Elizabeth Lambert Ortiz, Ruby Le Bois, Patricia Lousada, Norma MacMillan, Lesley Mackley, Sue Maggs, Sarah Maxwell, Maggie Mayhew, Jane Milton, Sallie Morris, Janice Murfitt, Annie Nichols, Angela Nilsen, Maggie Pannell, Keith Richmond, Anne Sheasby, Marlena Spieler, Liz Trigg, Hilaire Walden, Laura Washburn, Steven Wheeler, Jenny White, Kate Whiteman, Elizabeth Wolf-Cohencx

Home Economists Julie Beresford, Carla Capalbo, Kit Chan, Joanne Craig, Joanna Farrow, Annabel Ford, Nicola

Fowler, Christine France, Carole Handslip, Jane Hartshorn, Tonia Hedley, Shehzad Husain, Kate Jay, Becky Johnson, Wendy Lee, Sara Lewis, Lucy McKelvie, Annie Nichols, Bridget Sargeson, Jennie Shapter, Jane Stevenson, Sunil Vijayakar, Steven Wheeler, Elizabeth Wolf-Cohen.

Photographers Edward Allwright, Peter Anderson, David Armstrong, Steve Baxter, Martin Brigdale, Nicki Dowey, James Duncan, Gus Filgate, Michelle Garrett, Amanda Heywood, Janine Hosegood, Tim Hill, David Jordan, Dave King, Don Last, William Lingwood, Patrick McLeavey, Michael Michaels, Thomas Odulate, Peter Reilly, Craig Robertson, Simon Smith

Publisher: Joanna Lorenz
Senior Managing Editor:
    Conor Kilgallon
Editor: Lucy Doncaster
Designer: Bill Mason
Production Controller: Lee Sargent

A CIP catalogue record for this book is available from the British Library.

Previously published as part of a larger volume, *Low-Fat No-Fat Chinese Cooking*.